M000238215

The Book of Satanic Quotations

edited by
Matt G. Paradise

A Purging Talon Book

Copyright © 2008 by Matt G. Paradise

Published by Purging Talon
www.purgingtalon.com

ISBN: 978-0-6152-0368-3

All rights reserved. No part of this book may be used or reproduced in any manner whatsoever without written permission from the author, except in the case of brief quotations embodied in critical articles and reviews. For further information, address Purging Talon at info@purgingtalon.com

Cover and Book Design: Matt G. Paradise

Printed in the United States of America
Second Edition

Introduction

I have been a great collector of quotes since the first moment I opened a book and understood what was in front of me.

I was four years old when I consciously decided that reading was something I wanted to be able to do -- though, perhaps not for the more common reasons young children possess. Even still, I was quite compelled. Not by a desire to impress my parents or to merely amuse myself but by a rather adult observation: that knowledge is power in our culture and that accessing that power began with mastery of the written word. I was convinced, rightfully so, that there was something so indescribably important about all of this, and at the end of it all, power. It's safe to say that I was *very* interested in power, even at four.

Although I was certainly entertained by tales of fantasy and faraway lands -- full of vengeful genies, rodent wizards, wicked witches, and the list goes on -- my grade school years were also spent devouring books far beyond the reading comprehension standard for my age at the time. At six, I was reading murder mysteries, encyclopedias, and news magazine articles. At nine, it was adult historical fiction. And by 13, I had made my way through the works of Nietzsche, Machiavelli, Jung, Freud, and many of the other books on psychology, sexuality, and philosophy that literally lined the walls of my childhood home. So, when I had finally read *The Satanic Bible* at 15, it wasn't hard to figure out that both its author and I embraced quite a few relatable concepts from literature's past. So many of the quotes I'd mentally gathered throughout my life up until that point had been neatly reworded, intellectually expanded upon, and collected in one remarkable and workable religion / philosophy...

Satanism.

Enter a religion whose very principles are based upon pragmatism -- taking what works in life and discarding the rest. As a result, we are the consummate epicureans. This is why, for example, a Satanist might enjoy the organ/choral work of Bach yet has no concern that it is historically considered "church music." Ragnar Redbeard had some marvelous views regarding "rights" and the human will, but one doesn't need to abandon that because his major work also contains racist overtones. Even the innovative and breathtaking film work of Leni Riefenstahl can be enjoyed without getting needlessly worked up over her personal connection to Adolf Hitler and the Third Reich. In other words: toss the bathwater, keep the baby.

A good quote is of the same breed. And it's this mindful distillation that makes the difference between a grounded and informative collection of quotations and a book clumsily plastered with outdated sentiments and other filler.

Unfortunately, the latter is what passes for many a quotations book in current availability. Thumbing through one can often be like perusing many of them: the same, predictable pandering to Christianized thought with only a passing glance at really insightful, thought-provoking and iconoclastic ideas. For example, looking up "ethics" in your average quotes book reveals a rather forced relationship with such myopic and two-dimensional concepts as egalitarianism, the myth of equality, mindlessly loving your "neighbor," *et cetera ad nauseam.* In the end, much of it translates to simple-minded mediocrity -- no passion, no style, *no horns*!

And yet, even through all of the ages of transcribed ignorance and lip service paid to pious virtues, you could never really keep the Devil down. History is brimming to the point of overflow with Satanic philosophy, whether or not it carries that purportedly dread descriptive. Be it from familiar faces in school textbooks to celebrities of stage and screen to great individuals of science, literature, and politics, the eternal reminder of man's true carnal nature is deafening to those who have remained alert and aware in a consumer culture that otherwise demands unwavering obedience to its distractions. If while browsing through this collection you find yourself saying such things as "he said THAT!?" in response to many of the quotes, consider yourself -- perhaps, even momentarily -- undistracted.

And distractions are definitely everywhere, looking to reshape what you do, what you perceive, and what you say. Yes, even words are distractions, often playing upon the trifecta of inexperience, emotion, and groupthink.

Many folks who like to use the word, "religion" as a pejorative (and many in this book do just that) are really, though in a safely oblique way, denouncing Christianity. To a degree, the generalization is understandable because Christianity is the dominant religion in America and, the further you go back in our nation's history, the more impact it had. For over three centuries, this specific religion and its disastrously vague book have been a major source of antagonism and suppression from sea to shining sea. After all, it isn't the Buddhists in America who are crying out for the condemnation of homosexuals, liberals, divorcées, condom users and various other blasphemers. The Hindus among us aren't covertly taking over public office and attempting to institute their beliefs as secular law. And even the Jews in the United States aren't bombing abortion clinics, harassing or belittling those who don't believe as they do, or demanding that all of our children be made to study "intelligent design" or "creation science" in the schools. All of this and more exclusively comprises the grim legacy of Christianity in the Western world. (The Middle East has Islam to worry about, but that's largely *their* problem -- for now.) From crusades and inquisitions to apocalyptic cults and media censorship, what one questionably-existing "prophet" bequeathed to mankind over 2000 years ago has not been all flowers and lollipops. Credit where credit is due.

So, when you see the word, "religion" in the following quotes, it is often wise to keep a historical and cultural context in mind -- that the authors are often referring to the Christ religion specifically. But, also note that Christianity does not hold the patent on the word, either. In reality, religion and Christianity are not interchangeable terms -- something many "freethinking" Americans (and others as well) fail to consider when engaged in various knee-jerk responses to "the R word." The delusion process can be broken down as such: a) I don't like Christianity, b) Christianity is the only religion I know, c) Therefore, religion is bad. Even in atheistic circles, there is the propensity to default to all things counter-atheistic as being the fault of "religion." Sadly, even some of those godless heathens feel they are in need of a scapegoat.

In addition to Shinto, Sikhism, Confucianism, Taoism, and others mentioned, Satanism is also a religion -- albeit, a carnal one. And it might be agreeing with your natural world more than you might want to think. A lot more.

In a sense, it's likely that more than a few of the fine, upstanding citizens in this book had figuratively thrown their hands up in disgust and wondered where a religion based on both instinct and intellect was. Well, here it is! It's called Satanism, and it finds fault in many practices including deity-worship, self-abasement, mental slavery and abstaining from life in the here and now for some imagined afterlife that by all reasonable accounts doesn't exist. It's facts over fiction, life over lethargy, pleasure over pain. For the uninitiated, reading through these pages may just challenge some preconceptions and maybe even shatter a few outright lies. It's strange what can happen when someone actually opens a book and reads it.

It may also be fair to state that the mass of individuals in this book responsible for their quotes may or may not be Satanists, either admitted or in a *de facto* sense. Neither is necessarily important. In fact, in many cases, it's downright irrelevant. Good words can come from unexpected or even unintended sources. I included these quotes because they resonate with the Satanic philosophy and not for what their authors necessarily represented in their respective bodies of literature or their claimed affiliations as a whole.

Some of the individuals in this book are indeed Satanists, though. Not the least of which is the late Anton Szandor LaVey, founder of the Church of Satan (www.churchofsatan.com) and author of *The Satanic Bible*. LaVey synthesized a religion based on what I'd described in my previous book as "the reality of carnal existence and living one's life to its fullest, [which] rightfully champions mankind as being above his self-created gods and, as such, being totally responsible for his successes and failures." His books were not only filled with great observations on the human condition but also some choice book titles documented in either his indices or his body text (notably, in *The Satanic Witch*). Following suit, you might find the works from those quoted in *this* book equally stimulating and worthy of exploring further. Consider it a giant recommended reading list.

Also, there are probably quite a few people I simply overlooked for inclusion who may have deserved to be within these pages. Even in this Second Edition of the book, I still could not think of everyone in the known existence of man who said something thought-provoking, locate their works, and transcribe. So, I apologize to those who would have otherwise earned a place herein.

Throughout the last 20+ centuries, the Prince of Darkness has not only been the model of mindful rebellion but a grand orator, speak-

---

ing boldly and unrepentantly through the words of history's greatest thinkers and doers. He is the Black Flame that inspires man to think and move forward, in direct defiance of those who put superstition and other anti-human values at the forefront. He is mankind when man outgrows his silly spiritual fairy-tales and faces reality as a mature adult should. He is all of us when the alarm clock sounds.

And in that same metaphorical tradition, I present to you the Devil's most prominent advocates. Each quotation in this book becomes a burning trident sent straight through the hearts of those who vainly insist that man is anything but a carnal animal. Each sentiment, ablaze in glorious hellfire. And as each successive generation further abandons spirituality in greater and greater numbers in the 21st century, the inferno of rational thought will consume, cleanse, and bring forth its new children, a breed borne of true enlightenment and unencumbered by the fiction of God.

It is not only inevitable, it has already begun.

Hail knowledge! Hail Satan!

Magister Matt G. Paradise
11 April 2008

Edward Abbey
(1927-1989)

[a] God is a sound people make when they're too tired to think anymore.

[Vox Clamantis In Deserto]

Forrest J. Ackerman
(1916-   )

[b] I have not believed in God since childhood's end. I believe a belief in any deity is adolescent, shameful and dangerous. How would you feel, surrounded by billions of human beings taking Santa Claus, the Easter Bunny, the tooth fairy and the stork seriously, and capable of shaming, maiming or murdering in their name? I am embarrassed to live in a world retaining any faith in church, prayer or a celestial creator.

[The Faces Of Science Fiction]

Douglas Adams
(1952-2001)

[c] I really do not believe that there is a god, in fact I am convinced that there is not a god (a subtle difference), I see not a shred of evidence to suggest that there is one.

[American Atheism.
Winter, 1998-1999]

Henry Brooks Adams
(1838-1918)

[d] Knowledge of human nature is the beginning and end of political education.

[The Education of Henry Adams. Chap. 12]

[e] No one means all he says, and yet very few say all they mean, for words are slippery and thought is viscous.

[Ibid. Chap. 31]

John Adams
(1735-1826)

[f] I almost shudder at the thought of alluding to the most fatal example of the abuses of grief which the history of mankind has preserved -- the Cross. Consider what calamities that engine of grief has produced.

[letter to Thomas Jefferson]

[g] ...the government of the United States of America is not, in any sense, founded on the Christian Religion...

[Treaty Of Peace And Friendship With Tripoli,
Article XI]

John Quincy Adams
(1767-1848)

[h] My wants are many, and, if told, would muster many a score; and were each wish a mint of gold, I still should long for more.

[The Wants of Man, Stanza 1]

Samuel Adams
(1722-1803)

[i] If you love wealth better than liberty, the tranquility of servitude better than the animating contest of freedom, go home from us in peace. We ask not your counsels or arms. Crouch down and lick the hands which feed you. May your chains set lightly

upon you and may posterity forget that ye were our countrymen.

[speech at the Philadelphia State House, 1 August 1776]

George Adamson
(1906-1989)

[j] A lion is not a lion if it is only free to eat, to sleep, and to copulate. It deserves to be free to hunt and to choose its own prey; to look for and find its own mate; to fight for and hold its own territory.

[unsourced]

Joseph Addison
(1672-1719)

[k] True happiness is of a retired nature, and an enemy to pomp and noise; it arises, in the first place, from the enjoyment of one's self; and, in the next, from the friendship and conversation of a few select companions.

[The Spectator. No. 15,
17 March 1711]

[l] A man that has a taste of musick, painting, or architecture, is like one that has another sense, when compared with such as have no relish of those arts.

[Ibid. No. 93, 16 June 1711]

Wayne Adkins
(1948-   )

[m] How do we choose between believing in Jesus, Bigfoot, leprechauns, witchcraft, Islam, alien abductions, the Tooth Fairy, gold at the end of the rainbow or the myriad other assertions that people have made over the course of human history? [Faith is] like rolling the dice and hoping you have placed your faith in a true proposition...

[unsourced]

Aesop
(Floruit 550 B.C.E.)

[n] Beware lest you lose the substance by grasping at the shadow.

[The Dog and the Shadow]

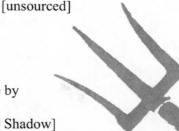

[o] Appearances are deceptive.

[The Wolf in Sheep's Clothing]

Alcaeus
(611-580 B.C.E.)

[p] 'Tis said that wrath is the last thing in a man to grow old.

[Scholiast on Sophocles]

Louisa May Alcott
(1832-1888)

[q] Resolved to take Fate by the throat and shake a living out of her.

[Letters and Journals, Chap. 3]

Ethan Allen
(1738-1789)

[r] While we are under the tyranny of Priests ... it will ever be their interest, to invalidate the law of nature and reason, in order to establish systems incompatible therewith.

[Reason the Only Oracle of Man, 1784]

[s] In those parts of the world where learning and science have prevailed, miracles have ceased; but in those parts of it as are barbarous and ignorant, miracles are still in vogue.

[Ibid.]

Al-Ma'arri
(973-1057)

[t] Do not suppose the statements of the prophets to be true. Men lived comfortably till they came and spoiled life. The "sacred books" are only such a set of idle tales as any age could have and indeed did actually produce.

[unsourced]

[u] If a man of sound judgment appeals to his intelligence, he will hold cheap the various

creeds and despise them. Do thou take thereof so much as Reason delivered (to thee), and let not ignorance plunge thee in their stagnant pool!

[unsourced]

Ferdinand Alquie
(1906-1985)

[v] The battle against the censure that hinders us from knowing ourselves will never be waged to the full unless we decide to attack it, not only in its moral structure, but also in its alliance with a reality principle, the plainest effect of which is keeping subjective and objective from rejoining.

[The Philosophy of Surrealism]

Henri-Frédéric Amiel
(1821-1881)

[w] A man without passion is only a latent force, only a possibility, like a stone waiting for the blow from the iron to give forth sparks.

[Journal]

[x] A belief is not true because it is useful.

[Journal Intime, 15 November 1876]

Sir Norman Angell
(1873-1967)

[y] The power of words is such that they have prevented our learning some of the most important events in the world's history.

[Let The People Know. Chap. 7]

Natalie Angier
(1958-   )

[z] ...the current climate of religiosity can be stifling to nonbelievers, and it helps now and then to cry foul. For one thing, some of the numbers surrounding the deep religiousness of America, and the rarity of nonbelief, should be held to the fire of skepticism, as should sweeping statistics of any sort.

["Confessions of a Lonely Atheist," in
New York Times Magazine, 14 January 2001]

Susan B. Anthony
(1820-1906)

[a] I distrust those people who know so well what God wants them to do because I notice it always coincides with their own desires.

[1896]

Aristotle
(384-322 B.C.E.)

[b] A tyrant must put on the appearance of uncommon devotion to religion. Subjects are less apprehensive of illegal treatment from a ruler whom they consider god-fearing and pious. On the other hand, they do less easily move against him, believing that he has the gods on his side.

[Politics]

[c] Even when laws have been written down, they ought not always to remain unaltered.

[Politics. Book II]

[d] That judges of important causes should hold office for life is not a good thing, for the mind grows old as well as the body.

[Ibid.]

[e] Prayers and sacrifices are of no avail.

[unsourced]

[f] Men create gods after their own image, not only with regard to their form but with regard to their mode of life.

[unsourced]

Karen Armstrong
(1944-   )

[g] If God is seen as a self in a world of his own, an ego that relates to a thought, a cause separate from its effect, "he" becomes a being,

not Being itself. An omnipotent, all-knowing tyrant is not so different from earthly dictators who make everything and everybody mere cogs in the machine which they controlled.

[A History of God]

Matthew Arnold
(1822-1888)

[h] Yet they, believe me, who await no gifts from Chance, have conquered Fate.

[Resignation]

[i] Resolve to be thyself: and know, that he who finds himself, loses his misery.

[Self-Dependence. Stanza 8]

Alan Ashley-Pitt
(?-?)

[j] The man who follows the crowd will usually get no further than the crowd. The man who walks alone is likely to find himself in places no one has ever been.

[unsourced]

Isaac Asimov
(1920-1992)

[k] Imagine the people who believe such things and who are not ashamed to ignore, totally, all the patient findings of thinking minds through all the centuries since the Bible was written. And it is these ignorant people, the most uneducated, the most unimaginative, the most unthinking among us, who would make themselves the guides and leaders of us all; who would force their feeble and childish beliefs on us; who would invade our schools and libraries and homes.
[Canadian Atheists Newsletter, 1994]

[l] Although the time of death is approaching me, I am not afraid of dying and going to Hell or (what would be considerably worse) going to the popularized version of Heaven. I

expect death to be nothingness and, for removing me from all possible fears of death, I am thankful to atheism.

["On Religiosity"]

[m] It is precisely because it is fashionable for Americans to know no science, even though they may be well educated otherwise, that they so easily fall prey to nonsense. They thus become part of the armies of the night, the purveyors of nitwittery, the retailers of intellectual junk food, the feeders on mental cardboard, for their ignorance keeps them from distinguishing nectar from sewage.

[The Armies Of The Night]

[n] Creationists make it sound as though a 'theory' is something you dreamt up after being drunk all night.

[As quoted in Like Rolling Uphill: Realizing the Honesty of Atheism by Dianna Narciso, p. 117]

**Athenaeus
(ca. 200)**

[o] It was a saying of Demetrius Phalereus, that "Men having often abandoned what was visible for the sake of what was uncertain, have not got what they expected, and have lost what they had -- being unfortunate by an enigmatical sort of calamity."

[The Deipnosophists. VI, 23]

**Peter William Atkins
(1940-   )**

[p] My aim is to argue that the universe can come into existence without intervention, and that there is no need to invoke the idea of a Supreme Being in one of its numerous manifestations.

[The Creation]

[q] Someone with a fresh mind, one not conditioned by upbringing and environment, would doubtless look at science and the powerful reductionism that it inspires as overwhelmingly the better mode of understanding the world, and would doubtless scorn religion

as sentimental wishful thinking. Would not that same uncluttered mind also see the attempts to reconcile science and religion by disparaging the reduction of the complex to the simple as attempts guided by muddle-headed sentiment and intellectually dishonest emotion?

["The Limitless Power of Science" essay in Nature's Imagination, John Cornwell, ed.; 1995 Oxford University Press, p.123]

Sir Francis Bacon
(1561-1626)

[r] Knowledge is power.

[Meditations Sacræ,
De Hæresibus]

[s] Truth can never be reached by just listening to the voice of an authority.
[unsourced]

[t] Atheism leaves a man to sense, to philosophy, to natural piety, to laws, to reputation, all which may be guides to an outward moral virtue... but superstition dismounts all these, and erecteth an absolute monarchy in the minds of men.

[The Essayes or Counsels,
Civill and Morall]

Philip James Bailey
(1816-1902)

[u] The first and worst of all frauds is to cheat oneself.

[Festus. Anywhere]

[v] The sole equality on earth is death.
[Ibid. A Country Town]

Carolyn Baker
(ca. 1945-   )

[w] Axiomatic in the worldview of the fundamentalist, born-again Christian is: "I have the truth, I'm right; you don't have the truth, you're wrong." As a result, critical thinking, research, or intellectual freedom of exploration are not only unnecessary, they are dangerous and potentially heretical... Moreover, because of one's "superior" spiritual status, one has the so-called "divine authority" to subvert, by whatever means necessary, the very machinery of government in order to establish a theocracy in which one's worldview is predominant.

[Scoop Independent News, 12 May 2005]

[x] The convert to fundamentalist Christianity must be convinced that his / her thinking is irreparably in error. The underlying message is: "You don't believe the Bible is the inerrant Word of God because your mind has been occupied by Satan. This has happened principally because you are a human being, but also because you have made the enormous mistake of trying to think for yourself. Of course you think there are contradictions in the Bible because Satan controls your mind..."

[Online Journal, 19 May 2005]

Mikhail Bakunin
(1814-1876)

[y] If God did exist, he would have to be abolished.

[God And The State]

[z] But here steps in Satan, the eternal rebel, the first free-thinker and emancipator of worlds. He makes man ashamed of his bestial ignorance and obedience; he emancipates him, stamps upon his brow the seal of liberty and humanity, in urging him to disobey and eat of the fruit of knowledge.

[Ibid.]

[a] The liberty of man consists solely in this: that he obeys natural laws because he has himself recognized them as such, and not because they have been externally imposed upon him by any extrinsic will whatever, di-

vine or human, collective or individual.

[Ibid.]

[b] All religions, with their gods, their demi-gods, and their prophets, their messiahs and their saints, were created by the prejudiced fancy of men who had not attained the full development and full possession of their faculties.

[Ibid.]

[c] God, or rather the fiction of God, is thus the sanction and the intellectual and moral cause of all the slavery on earth, and the liberty of men will not be complete, unless it will have completely annihilated the inauspicious fiction of a heavenly master.

[Oeuvres]

[d] The idea of God implies the abdication of human reason and justice; it is the most decisive negation of human liberty and necessarily ends in the enslavement of mankind both in theory and practice. He who desires to worship God must harbor no childish illusions about the matter but bravely renounce his liberty and humanity.

[Federalism, Socialism, and Anti-Theologism]

[e] We are materialists and atheists, and we glory in the fact.

[unsourced]

**Dan Barker
(1949-   )**

[f] Faith is a cop-out. It is intellectual bankruptcy. If the only way you can accept an assertion is by faith, then you are conceding that it can't be taken on its own merits.

[Losing Faith In Faith: From Preacher To Atheist]

[g] You can cite a hundred references to show that the biblical God is a bloodthirsty tyrant, but if they can dig up two or three verses that say "God is love" they will claim that you are taking things out of context!

[Ibid.]

[h] Freethinkers reject faith as a valid tool of

knowledge. Faith is the opposite of reason because reason imposes very strict limits on what can be true, and faith has no limits at all. A Great Escape into faith is no retreat to safety. It is nothing less than surrender.

[Ibid.]

[i] The very concept of sin comes from the Bible. Christianity offers to solve a problem of its own making! Would you be thankful to a person who cut you with a knife in order to sell you a bandage?

[Ibid.]

[j] Basic atheism is not a belief. It is the lack of belief. There is a difference between believing there is no god and not believing there is a god -- both are atheistic, though popular usage has ignored the latter.

[quoted from Austin Cline,
"Defining Atheism: Contemporary Atheists"]

Phineas Taylor Barnum
(1810-1891)

[k] There's a sucker born every minute.

[unsourced]

Blanche Barton
(?-   )

[l] In all ways, Satanists deal exclusively with dark, unexplored realms. They speak the unspeakable, challenge the indisputable, and refuse to bow down before established icons.

[The Church of Satan]

[m] There's a rich heresy and blasphemy behind it [Satanism], but as far as an aboveground religion that reveres Satan, there wasn't anything before the Church of Satan's foundation in 1966.

[interview from Lucifer Rising by
Gavin Baddeley, pp. 219, 220]

[n] Satan has always represented and will always represent the adversary. He is a counterbalance to the unspoken injustice that prevails

in the current society, whether that be overweening elitism or, going to the opposite extreme, mob rule. We always have to be in the minority that push hard in the other direction to get the pendulum swinging. Satanism will never be a religion of the people.

[Ibid.]

[o] Apply your enthusiasm toward larger practical goals... We [Satanists] are responsible for the Renaissance, the revolution, if there is to be any at all. We are the leaders, not the gossips, critics and commentators... Don't get bogged down in networking and he-said/she-said accusations, spending so much time playing the game we lose sight of the objective. Examine motives, not smokescreen "issues."

["Sycophants Unite" from The Black Flame. Vol. 5, #s 3 & 4]

[p] ...schools are designed to make you complacent, homogenized and to extinguish any spark of curiosity or willfulness you may possess... Today, children are taught the moral value of getting up at 7 a.m. every morning, going to a place you don't want to be, with a lot of people you'd consider your inferiors to take instructions from someone you can't respect.

["Mandatory Education: Teaching Pigs To Sing" from
The Black Flame. Vol. 5, #s 3 & 4]

[q] Satanists have an innate complexity of mind that hungers for uncompromising examination and speculation, not superficially-comforting pap. We don't need to be comforted; we prefer the invigorating, bracing wind of truth and terror.

["Satanic Feminism" from The Black Flame. Vol. 6, #s 1 & 2]

[r] Satanic women don't want to gain their strength by castrating men, or by making themselves out as victims. Whether they're providing healing and inspiration to those under their roofs, cracking the whip in corporate circles, managing their own home-based businesses or maneuvering whatever they need to survive, all are applying and increasing their power -- not whining about why they don't have any!

[Ibid.]

[s] Nature provides variations in genetic encoding in hopes of developing a better strain. Some changes weaken, others strengthen. When

natural processes hit upon something that will strengthen the breed, natural selection guarantees this aberration will survive. If we [Satanists] are indeed the next evolution of the human race, possessors of that rare genetic information which will create a stronger, more resilient creature for all our tomorrows, it emboldens us to protect that which sets us apart. For the ideals and attitudes we have cannot be dissipated in deference to the majority...

["All Satanists Look Alike To Me..."
from The Cloven Hoof. Vol. XIX, #1. Issue 115]

[t] One main point of Satanism is that it demands self-sufficiency. People that are looking for friends, or followers, or fancy titles, false hope or magical carrot-dangling need not apply.

["Renaissance' from The Cloven Hoof. Issue 126]

[u] Our history books are being quickly rewritten to accommodate minority concerns. This is a serious threat -- to the way we think, the way we feel about ourselves and, of primary importance to magicians, to the language of archetypes we all hold consistent. It is the beginning of all unreason if we wipe out our knowledge of the past.

["Wicca: Exposed! (and Exorcised)" from The Cloven Hoof. Issue 127]

[v] ...the uncomprehending questions finally comes: "Well, that all sounds great. But why do you have to call it Satanism? You know, you'd probably get a lot more followers if you called it something else -- like Humanism or Atheism." ...How can you explain that that is exactly why we call it Satanism? Because it is the word that separates the sheep from the wolves. No matter how liberated and non-judgmental they claim to be, if they can't get past that simple, two-syllable word, their minds are still enslaved. We are eternally separated by that one word, Satan.

["The Power of the Name" from The Cloven Hoof. Issue 127]

[w] Satan is the patron of all that is unfashionable. By definition, our perspective, opinions and priorities are more than a bit different from most people's -- and we take great pride in that fact... By dint of genetic predisposition, we are not like everybody else.

["Thirteen Eugenic and Environmental Departures Toward a New Satanic Ethnic" from The Cloven Hoof. Issue 128]

[x] We [as Satanists] recognize and despise the stupidity, illogic, complacency, pretentiousness and blind self-righteousness that Christianity and other spiritual religions breed. The attitudes and beliefs they spread are unnatural to humans and cancerous to society. Satanists exist in every culture, by many different names, as the ones who challenge authority and question the status quo. As such, Satanists will always be the subject of fascination and speculation.

[Ibid.]

[y] Most people don't really want to think independently or make decisions; they're herd animals with herd instincts to keep to the middle of the group where it's safest, don't stand out too much, don't move too far away from convention, etc. They want to be led and dictated to. But they're stubborn, mulish animals and they like to think they're independent and free.

[Ibid.]

[z] Satanism is unique as a religion in that it is not inherently incompatible with science. Most religions are antagonistic to science, since their premises are based on spiritual "truths" that must be accepted on faith. Satanism is not based on revelation or articles of faith -- it is based on reason, pragmatism and tangible indulgence.

["Of Scientists and Satanists" from The Cloven Hoof. Issue 128]

[a] Civilization isn't a right. It is earned by each of us each morning we wake up and decide we will not kill without provocation, we will not steal, rape or harm the innocent. We will endeavor to be productive and justify our existence.

["The Grand Conspiracy" from The Cloven Hoof. Issue 129]

[b] If... we see Satanism as more than just a set of rational guidelines for everyday interactions, it implies that we will use its symbology to communicate our cultural values to generations beyond us.

["Is Satanism a Religion?" from
The Cloven Hoof. Issue 129]

[c] ...Satanism is very practical and pragmatic. It most certainly contains values that can encourage and sustain us as individuals, as families, and as communities. The archetypes we align ourselves with evoke courage

and concentration. Ours is no more than the same commonsense wisdom that people have depended on for centuries, minus self-righteous self-deceit.

[Ibid.]

Charles Baudelaire
(1821-1867)

[d] Glory and praise be with you, Satan, in the heights
Of the Sky, where you reigned, and in the lightless nights
Of Hell, where now, overcome, you dream in silence!
May my heart, one day, under the Tree of Science,
Rest close to you, at the hour when around your head
A new Temple will rise and its branches will spread!

[Litanies To Satan]

[e] God is the only being who, in order to reign, doesn't even need to exist.

[unsourced]

Pakenham Beatty
(Floruit 1881)

[f] By thine own soul's law learn to live,
And if men thwart thee, take no heed,
And if men hate thee, have no care;
Sing thou thy song, and do thy deed,
Hope thou thy hope, and pray thy prayer.

[Self-Reliance. Stanza 1]

Francis Beaumont
(1584-1616)

[g] What's one man's poison, signor, is another's meat or drink.

[Love's Cure. Act III, Sc. 2]

Simone de Beauvoir
(1908-1986)

[h] All the idols made by man, however terrifying they may be, are in point of fact subor-
dinate to him, and that is why he will always

have it in his power to destroy them.

[The Second Sex]

[i] I cannot be angry at God, in whom I do not believe.

[The Observer (London), 7 January 1979]

August Bebel
(1840-1913)

[j] Christianity is the enemy of liberty and of civilization. It has kept mankind in chains.

[Reichstag speech,
31 March 1881]

[k] Christ came, and Christianity arose... But originating in Judaism, which knew woman only as a being bereft of all rights, and biased by the Biblical conception which saw in her the source of all evil, Christianity preached contempt for women.

[Woman and Socialism]

Cesare Beccaria
(1738-1794)

[l] Laws that forbid the carrying of arms disarm only those who are neither inclined nor determined to commit crimes. Such laws make things worse for the assaulted and better for the assailants; they serve rather to encourage than prevent homicides, for an unarmed man may be attacked with greater confidence than an armed man.

[On Crimes and
Punishment]

John Beevers
(1911-1975)

[m] I do not know that Christianity holds anything more of importance for the world. It is finished, played out. The only trouble lies in how to get rid of the body before it begins to smell too much.

[World Without Faith]

Gerald L. Berry
(?-?)

[n] About 200 B.C. mystery cults began to appear in Rome just as they had earlier in Greece. Most notable was the Cybele cult centered on Vatican hill... Associated with the Cybele cult was that of her lover, Attis (the older Tammuz, Osiris, Dionysus, or Orpheus under a new name). He was a god of ever-reviving vegetation. Born of a virgin, he died and was reborn annually. The festival began as a day of blood on Black Friday and culminated after three days in a day of rejoicing over the resurrection.

[Religions of the World]

Matt Berry
(?-?)

[o] Faith is the fatigue resulting from the attempt to preserve God's integrity instead of one's own.

[Post-Atheism]

[p] ...one can be happier and more valuable without a "beyond" ...that one can not only learn to be content with reality, but can aggressively pursue greater and greater joy.

[A Human Strategy]

Annie Wood Besant
(1847-1933)

[q] Never yet has a God been defined in terms which were not palpably self-contradictory and absurd...

[Why I Do Not Believe in God]

[r] If my interlocutor desires to convince me that Jupiter has inhabitants, and that his description of them is accurate, it is for him to bring forward evidence in support of his contention. The burden of proof evidently lies on him; it is not for me to prove that no such beings exist before my non-belief is justified, but for him to prove that they do exist before my belief can be fairly claimed. Similarly, it is for the affirmer of God's existence to bring

evidence in support of his affirmation; the burden of proof lies on him.

[Ibid.]

Jello Biafra
(1957-   )

[s] I think all empires must collapse when they get too comfortable, and this empire's collapsing before our very eyes. It's really a very interesting form of vaudeville, and a hideous form at that.

[Maximum Rocknroll. 1983]

[t] ...I see pranks more as a social and moral obligation. Anybody can be a good Boy Scout and do their prankish deed at least once a day and feel cleansed and better as a result.

[interview from RE/Search: Pranks!]

Ambrose Bierce
(1842-1914)

[u] Faith: Belief without evidence in what is told by one who speaks without knowledge, of things without parallel.

[The Devil's Dictionary]

[v] Pray: To ask the laws of the universe to be annulled on behalf of a single petitioner confessedly unworthy.

[Ibid.]

[w] I don't believe in the greatest good to the greatest number. It seems to me perfect rot. I believe in the greatest good to the best man. And I would sacrifice a hundred incapable men to elevate one really great man.

[as quoted in With Charity Toward None
by Florence King]

Josh Billings
(Henry Wheeler Shaw)
(1818-1885)

[x] Better to make a weak man your enemy than your friend.

[Affurisms]

Björk
(1965-   )

[y] Iceland sets a world-record. The United Nations asked people from all over the world a series of questions. Iceland stuck out on one thing. When we were asked what do we believe, 90% said, "ourselves." I think I'm in that group. If I get into trouble, there's no God or Allah to sort me out. I have to do it myself.

[HotPress. 1994]

William Blake
(1757-1827)

[z] As the caterpillar chooses the fairest leaves to lay her eggs on, so the priest lays his curse on the fairest joys.

[Proverbs of Hell]

[a] I care not whether man is good or evil; all that I care
Is whether he is a wise man or a fool. Go, put off holiness
And put on intellect...

[Jerusalem]

[b] I must create a system or be enslaved by another man's. I will not reason and compare; My business is to create.

[The Marriage of Heaven and Hell]

Howard Bloom
(1943-   )

[c] Lucifer is almost everything men like Milton imagined him to be. He is ambitious, an organizer, a force reaching out vigorously to master even the stars of heaven. But he is not a demon separate from Nature's benevolence. He is a part of the creative force itself.

[The Lucifer Principle]

Wilfred Scawen Blunt
(1840-1922)

[d] Nor has the world a better thing, though

one should search it round, than thus to live one's own sole king, upon one's own sole ground.

[The Old Squire. Stanza 14]

William Bolitho
(1890-1930)

[e] His real glory is that of all adventurers: to have been the tremendous outsider.

[Twelve Against the Gods]

Napoleon Bonaparte
(1769-1821)

[f] All religions have been made by men.

[letter to Gaspard Gourgaud, 28 January 1817]

[g] The bullet that will kill me is not yet cast.

[At Montereau. 1814]

[h] Madame Montholon having inquired what troops he considered the best, "Those which are victorious, Madame," replied the Emperor.

[Bourrienne: Memoirs, Vol. 10, p. 399]

[i] A soul? Give my watch to a savage, and he will think it has a soul.

[unsourced]

Jorge Luis Borges
(1899-1986)

[j] [Christianity] belongs to the history of Jewish su-perstitions.

["Death and the Compass"]

James Boswell
(1740-1795)

[k] That favorite subject, Myself.

[Letter to Temple, 26 July 1763]

G. Richard Bozarth
(1949-   )

[l] Christianity has fought, still fights, and will fight science to the desperate end over evolution, because evolution destroys utterly and finally the very reason Jesus' earthly life was supposedly made necessary. Destroy Adam and Eve and the original sin, and in the rubble you will find the sorry remains of the son of God.

[American Atheist, Feb. 1978]

Ray Bradbury
(1920-   )

[m] There is more than one way to burn a book. And the world is full of people running around with lit matches. Every minority... feels it has the will, the right, the duty to douse the kerosene, light the fuse. Every dimwit editor who sees himself as the source of all dreary blanc-mange plain porridge un-leavened literature, licks his guillotine and eyes the neck of any author who dares to speak above a whisper or write above a nursery rhyme.

[Fahrenheit 451. Afterword]

[n] For it is a mad world and it will get madder if we allow the minorities, be they dwarf or giant, orangutan or dolphin, nuclear-head or water-conserva-tionist, pro-computerologist or Neo-Luddite, simpleton or sage, to interfere with aesthetics.

[Ibid.]

Charles Bradlaugh
(1833-1891)

[o] If special honor is claimed for any, then heresy should have it as the truest servitor of humankind.

[25 September 1881]

[p] The atheist does not say "there is no God" but he says "I do not know what you mean by God; I am without the idea of God; the word God is to me a sound conveying no clear or distinct affirmation. I do not deny God, because I cannot deny that of which I

have no conception and the conception of which by its affirmer is so imperfect that he is unable to define it to me."

[National Review,
25 November 1883]

[q] I cannot follow you Christians; for you try to crawl through your life upon your knees, while I stride through mine on my feet.

[unsourced]

Berton Braley
(1882-?)

[r] With doubt and dismay you are smitten, you think there's no chance for you, son? Why, the best books haven't been written, the best race hasn't been run.

[Opportunity. Stanza 1]

[s] If with pleasure you are viewing any work a man is doing, if you like him or you love him, tell him now. Do not wait till life is over and he's underneath the clover, for he cannot read his tombstone when he's dead!

[Do It Now.
Stanzas 1 and 2]

Anna Hempstead Branch
(1875-1937)

[t] Order is a lovely thing; on disarray it lays its wing, teaching simplicity to sing.

[The Monk in
the Kitchen]

André Breton
(1896-1966)

[u] I have always wagered against God and...
I am conscious of having won to the full.
Everything that is doddering, squint-eyed,
vile, polluted and grotesque is summoned up
for me in that one word: God!

[Surrealism and Painting]

Emily Brontë
(1818-1848)

[v] I'll walk where my own nature would be leading -- It vexes me to choose another guide -- Where the grey flocks in ferny glens are feeding, where the wild wind blows on the mountain-side.

[Often Rebuked.
Stanza 4]

David Marshall Brooks
(1902-1994)

[w] To explain the unknown by the known is a logical procedure; to explain the known by the unknown is a form of theological lunacy.

[The Necessity of Atheism]

James A.C. Brown
(1911-1964)

[x] Propaganda by censorship takes two forms: the selective control of information to favour a particular viewpoint, and the deliberate doctoring of information in order to create an impression different from that originally intended.

[Techniques Of Persuasion, 1963]

Michael H. Brown
(1942-   )

[y] You've got to know where the machinery is and how it works before you can throw a monkey-wrench into it.

[Brown's Lawsuit Cookbook]

Trevor Brown
(?-   )

[z] I'm not deliberately setting out to offend the morally righteous, and I also do not see myself a martyr exploring the dark side of human existence. I'm interested in this whole area of crossing of wires and short-circuiting

predictable programmed responses.

[interview from Juxtapoz Erotica #2]

Lenny Bruce
(1925-1966)

[a] People should be taught what is, not what should be.

[quoted from Dr. Keith Semmel, "Stand-Up Comics and Religion"]

Giordano Bruno
(1548-1600)

[b] It is proof of a base and low mind for one to wish to think with the masses or majority, merely because the majority is the majority. Truth does not change because it is, or is not, believed by a majority of the people.

[Heroic Furies]

Pearl S. Buck
(1892-1973)

[c] Be born anywhere, little embryo novelist, but do not be born under the shadow of a great creed, not under the burden of original sin, not under the doom of Salvation.

[Advice To Unborn Novelists]

[d] I am so absorbed in the wonder of earth and the life upon it that I cannot think of heaven and the angels. I have enough for this life.

[Treasury of Women's Quotations]

Henry Thomas Buckle
(1821-1862)

[e] As long as men refer the movements of the comets to the immediate finger of God, and as long as they believe that an eclipse is one of the modes by which the deity expresses his anger, they will never be guilty of the blasphemous presumption of attempting to predict such supernatural appearances. Before they could dare to investigate the causes of

these mysterious phenomena, it is necessary that they should believe, or at all events that they should suspect, that the phenomena themselves were capable of being explained by the human mind.

[History Of Civilization, vol I]

E.A. Wallis Budge
(1857-1934)

[f] ... it is clear that the early Christians bestowed some of her [Isis'] attributes upon the Virgin Mary. There is little doubt that in her character of the loving and protecting mother she appealed strongly to the imagination of all the Eastern peoples among whom her cult came, and that the pictures and sculptures wherein she is represented in the act of suckling her child Horus formed the foundation for the Christian figures and paintings of the Madonna and Child. Several of the incidents of the wanderings of the Virgin with the child in Egypt as recorded in the Apocryphal Gospels reflect scenes in the life of Isis as described in the texts found on the Metternich Stele, and many of the attributes of Isis, the God-mother, the mother of Horus, and of Neith, the goddess of Saïs, are identical with those of Mary the Mother of Christ.

[The Gods Of The Egyptians, Vol. 2, 1904]

Luis Buñuel
(1900-1983)

[g] To many people a personal code is a childish thing, but not to me. I am against conventional morality -- all our traditional illusions, sentimentality, and the moral filth of society that is engendered by sentimentality... It is the morality that is founded on our most unjust social institutions, like religion, fatherland, family, culture -- everything that people call the "pillars" of society.

[quoted in RE/Search: Pranks!]

Luther Burbank
(1849-1926)

[h] I have learned from Nature that dependence on unnatural beliefs weakens us in the struggle and shortens our breath for the race.

[quoted from Joseph Lewis, Burbank the Infidel]

[i] The idea that a good God would send people to a burning hell is utterly damnable to me. The ravings of insanity! Superstition gone to seed! I don't want to have anything to do with such a God.

[reported in Edgar Waite's "Luther Burbank, Infidel"]

[j] I do not believe what has been served to me to believe. I am a doubter, a questioner, a skeptic. However, when it can be proved to me that there is immortality, that there is resurrection beyond the gates of death, then will I believe. Until then, no.

[Ibid.]

Edmund Burke
(1729-1797)

[k] Kings will be tyrants from policy, when subjects are rebels from principle.

[Reflections on the Revolution in France]

[l] He that wrestles with us strengthens our nerves and sharpens our skill. Our antagonist is our helper.

[Ibid.]

[m] Superstition is the religion of feeble minds.

[unsourced]

Robert Burns
(1759-1796)

[n] Gie me ae spark o' Nature's fire, that's a' the learning I desire.

[First Epistle to J. Lapraik. Stanza 13]

[o] Morality, thou deadly bane, thy tens o' thousands thou hast slain!

[A Dedication to Gavin Hamilton]

[p] But my downcast eye by chance did spy
What made my lips to water,
Those limbs so clean where I, between,
Commenc'd a Fornicator.

[unsourced]

Richard Francis Burton
(1821-1890)

[q] There is no Heaven, there is no Hell;
These are the dreams of baby minds;
Tools of the wily Fetisheer,
To fright the fools his cunning blinds.

[The Kasidah]

[r] Do what thy manhood bids thee do,
from none but self expect applause:
He noblest lives and noblest dies
who makes and keeps his self-made laws.

[Ibid.]

[s] There is no Good, there is no Bad;
these be the whims of mortal will:
What works for me weal that call I 'good,'
what harms and hurts I hold as 'ill...'

[Ibid.]

Samuel Butler
(1835-1902)

[t] Prayers are to men as dolls are to children. They are not without use and comfort, but it is not easy to take them seriously.

[Notebooks, 1912]

[u] I really do not see much use in exalting the humble and meek; they do not remain humble and meek long when they are exalted.

[Ibid.]

Lord Byron
(1788-1824)

[v] In solitude, where we are least alone.
[Childe Harold's Pilgrimage, Canto III, Stanza 90]

[w] Among them, but not of them; in a shroud

of thoughts which were not their thoughts.

[Ibid, Stanza 113]

[x]   I tempt none,
Save with the truth: was not the tree, the tree
Of knowledge? and was not the tree of life
Still fruitful? Did I bid her pluck them not?
Did I plant things prohibited within
The reach of being innocent, and curious
By their own innocence? I would have made ye Gods: and even He who
thrust ye forth, so thrust ye Because ye should not eat the fruits of life, And
become the gods as We.

[Cain]

[y] I do not believe in any revealed religion. I will have nothing to do with
your immortality...

[letter to the Rev. Francis Hodgson, 1811]

**James Branch Cabell
(1879-1958)**

[z] Personally, I do not like human beings because I am not aware, upon the whole, of any generally distributed qualities which entitle them as a race to admiration and affection.

[Beyond Life]

[a] All democratic government... is of course based on the axiom that the man of average intelligence is in theory equal to a person of exceptional endowments, and in practice the superior by reason of numbers.

[Ibid.]

**Joseph Campbell
(1904-1987)**

[b] My favorite definition of religion is "a misrepresentation of mythology." And the misrepresentation consists precisely in attributing historical references to symbols which properly are spiritual in their reference.

[An Open Life, 1988]

[c] The night of December 25, to which date the Nativity of Christ was ultimately assigned, was exactly that of the birth of the Persian savior Mithra, who, as an incarnation of

eternal light, was born the night of the winter solstice (then dated December 25) at midnight, the instant of the turn of the year from increasing darkness to light.

[The Mythic Image, 1981]

[d] What gods are there, what gods have there ever been, that were not from man's imagination?

[Myths to Live By]

Thomas Campbell
(1777-1844)

[e] To live in hearts we leave behind is not to die.

[Hallowed Ground. Stanza 6]

Albert Camus
(1913-1960)

[f] In order to exist just once in the world, it is necessary never again to exist.

[The Rebel]

[g] If there is a sin against life, it consists perhaps not so much in despairing of life as in hoping for another life and in eluding the implacable grandeur of this life.

[The Myth of Sisyphus]

[h] Beware of those who say: "I know this too well to be able to express it." For if they cannot do so, this is because they don't know it or because out of laziness they stopped at the outer crust.

[The Absurd Man]

George Canning
(1770-1827)

[i] And finds, with keen, discriminating sight, black's not so black,-- nor white so very white.

[New Morality]

Giosuè Carducci
(1835-1907)

[j] I animate all who fight against servitude. The heroes and martyrs of liberty and progress in every age have drunk of my spirit. I inspire the revolter, the scorner, the skeptic, the satirist. I still distribute the tree of knowledge. I am the soul of the world. I am the lightning of the human mind. I level thrones and altars and annihilate binding customs. With a goad of restless aspirations I urge men on until they outgrow faith and fear...

[Hymn To Satan]

George Carlin
(1937-   )

[k] I would never want to be a member of a group whose symbol was a guy nailed to two pieces of wood.

[from the album, A Place For My Stuff]

[l] Nature should be allowed to do its job of killing off the weak and sickly and ignorant people without interference from airbags and batting helmets. Just think of it as passive eugenics.

[from the video, You Are All Diseased]

[m] Something is wrong here. War, disease, death, destruction, hunger, filth, poverty, torture, crime, corruption, and the Ice Capades. Something is definitely wrong. This is not good work. If this is the best God can do, I am not impressed. Results like these do not belong on the résumé of a Supreme Being. This is the kind of shit you'd expect from an office temp with a bad attitude. And just between you and me, in any decently-run universe, this guy would've been out on his all-powerful ass a long time ago.

[Ibid.]

[n] Religion easily has the greatest bullshit story ever told. Think about it, religion has actually convinced people that there's an INVISIBLE MAN... LIVING IN THE SKY... who watches every thing you do, every minute of every day. And the invisible man has a list of ten special things that he does not want

you to do. And if you do any of these ten things, he has a special place full of fire and smoke and burning and torture and anguish where he will send you to live and suffer and burn and choke and scream and cry forever and ever 'til the end of time... but he loves you.

[Brain Droppings]

Thomas Carlyle
(1795-1881)

[o] No man lives without jostling and being jostled; in all ways he has to elbow himself through the world, giving and receiving offence.

[London and Westminster Review. 12 November 1838]

[p] Be not the slave of Words.

[Sartor Resartus. Book I, Chap. 8]

[q] Just in the ratio that knowledge increases, faith diminishes.

[unsourced]

[r] If Jesus Christ were to come today, people would not even crucify him. They would ask him to dinner, and hear what he had to say, and make fun of him.

[unsourced]

[s] If I had my way, the world would hear a pretty stern command -- Exit Christ.

[unsourced]

James Earl "Jimmy" Carter, Jr.
(1924-   )

[t] The government ought to stay out of the prayer business.

[press conference, 1979, Washington, DC]

Paul Carus
(1852-1919)

[u] The Devil is the rebel of the cosmos, the independent in the empire of a tyrant, the

opposition to uniformity, the dissonance in universal harmony, the exception to the rule, the particular in the universal, the unforeseen chance that breaks the law; he is the individualizing tendency, the craving for originality, which bodily upsets the ordinances of God that enforce a definite kind of conduct; he overturns the monotony that would permeate the cosmic spheres if every atom in unconscious righteousness and with pious obedience slavishly followed a generally prescribed course.

[The History of the Devil
And The Idea of Evil]

[v] The early Christians belonged exclusively to the lower walks of life, and the earliest Church authorities, with few exceptions, were by no means cultured or highly educated persons... Thus it is natural that Christians were lacking both in knowledge as to the origin of many of their rites and also in critique, and when they were confronted with the same practices and conceptions among non-Christians, they were puzzled and found no other explanation for such remarkable coincidences, than the guiles of Satan.

[Ibid.]

[w] It was natural that heretics should always be regarded as belonging to the same category as witches and wizards, for they, too, according to the logic of ecclesiastical reasoning [were] "worshippers of Satan."

[Ibid.]

[x] He [the Devil] appears as the critic of the good Lord, as the representative of discontent with existing conditions, he inspires men with the desire for an increase of wealth, power and knowledge; he is the mouth-piece of all who are anxious for a change in matters political, social, and ecclesiastical. He is identified with the spirit of progress so inconvenient to those who are satisfied with the existing state of things, and thus he is credited with innovations of all kinds...

[Ibid.]

[y] Truly if we cannot have a religion which makes us free and independent, let us discard religion! Religion must be in accord not only with morality but also with philosophy; not only with justice, but also with science; not only with order, but also with freedom.

[Ibid.]

Jerry Casale
(1948-   )

[z] Often what you're doing [with pranksterism] is re-aligning people's associations with stimuli, which can even be pre-language. Basically we're dealing with a value system based on icons, objects, symbols, and situations that have a social status: a certain appropriate behavior in a situation. The prank takes all this into account, the way a movie will set you up.

[interview in RE/Search: Pranks!]

[a] A prank only victimizes to the degree that people are attached to their level of reality -- that's what it's really about. The more uptight and constipated someone is about their reality, the more the prank is offensive.

[Ibid.]

Celsus
(ca. late-100s)

[b] In all of these beliefs you have been deceived; yet you persist doggedly to seek justification for the absurdities you have made doctrines.

[On The True Doctrine]

[c] One ought first to follow reason as a guide before accepting any belief, since anyone who believes without testing a doctrine is certain to be deceived.

[Ibid.]

[d] There is nothing new or impressive about their [Christians'] ethical teaching; indeed, when one compares it to other philosophies, their simple-mindedness becomes apparent.

[Ibid.]

[e] Let's assume for a minute that he [Jesus] foretold his resurrection. Are you ignorant of the multitudes who have invented similar tales to lead simple minded hearers astray?

[Ibid.]

[f] The Christians babble about God day and night in their impious and sullied way; they

arouse the awe of the illiterate with their false descriptions of the punishments awaiting those who have sinned.

[Ibid.]

[g] Taking its [Christianity's] roots in the lower classes, the religion continues to spread among the vulgar: nay, one can even say it spreads because of its vulgarity, and the illiteracy of its adherents.

[Ibid.]

[h] So too their [Christianity's] fantastic story – which they take from the Jews – concerning the flood and the building of an enormous ark, and the business about the message being brought back to the survivors of the flood by a dove (or was it an old crow?). This is nothing more than a debased and nonsensical version of the myth of Deucalion, a fact I am sure they would not want to come light.

[Ibid.]

Miguel de Cervantes
(1547-1616)

[i] You are a King by your own Fireside, as much as any Monarch in his Throne.

[Don Quixote. Preface, page xix]

[j] To give the Devil his due.

[Ibid. Page 111]

[k] Paid him in his own coin.

[Ibid. Page 121]

[l] Ne'er cringe nor creep, for what you by force may reap.
[Ibid. Page 149]

Charlie Chaplin
(1889-1977)

[m] Dictators free themselves by enslaving others. They work not for your benefit, but their own.
[from the movie, "The Little Dictator"]

[n] By simple common sense I don't believe in God, in none.

[unsourced]

George Chatterton-Hill
(?-?)

[o] It must ever be remembered that Christianity is an invention of the lowest classes, that it represents the ideal of those classes, that it alone benefits those classes. But its action must be restrained to the sphere of those whose ideal it is. The slaves, the oppressed, the weak, the outcast, the mediocrities, can find satisfaction in Christianity. It is not the duty of the masters to deny them that satisfaction. But the masters have their own ideal, and an ideal which is diametrically and totally opposed to that of Christianity...

[The Philosophy of
Nietzsche]

[p] The Over-Man needs the masses under him, he needs them in order to subsist. The ordinary work of civilization, the drudgery and toil of life... requires a vast horde of workers, willing, laborious, obedient, of mediocre intelligence, diligent, unpretending.

[Ibid.]

G. K. Chesterton
(1874-1936)

[q] Fallacies do not cease to be fallacies because they become fashions.

[Illustrated London News,
19 April 1930]

[r] A dead thing can go with the stream, but only a living thing can go against it.

[Everlasting Man, 1925]

George William Childs
(1829-1894)

[s] Do not keep the alabaster boxes of your love and tenderness sealed up until your friends are dead. Fill their lives with sweetness. Speak approving, cheering words while

their ears can hear them, and while their hearts can be thrilled and made happier by them.

[A Creed]

"Diabolus Rex" Church
(1960-   )

[t] Each new creation of mine is a Sigil for change, to work my WILL upon the Universe... My work is that of the messenger, he who would throw open the gates to herald the entrance of the Lords of Chaos, the entities of change that will bend the universe to a new aesthetic.

[interview from The Black Pun-Kin
Vol. 4]

[u] I have never identified with race, culture or creed of any "human" type. The only "race" I have ever recognized is that of the demonic, and... it is held by some Satanists that humanity at large is not "human" but a flawed death-worshiping byproduct arising from false values (and slated for extinction)...

[Ibid.]

Winston Spencer Churchill
(1874-1965)

[v] Nothing in life is so exhilarating as to be shot at without result.

[The Malakand Field Force, 1898]

[w] Victory at all costs, victory in spite of all terror, victory however long and hard the road may be; for without victory there is no survival.

[First Statement as Prime Minister,
House of Commons, 13 May 1940]

[x] ...it is better to perish than to live as slaves.

[unsourced]

[y] Never give in, never give in, never, never, never, never -- in nothing, great or small, large or petty -- never give in except to convictions of honor and good sense.

[Address at Harrow School,
29 October 1941]

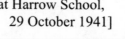

Emil M. Cioran
(1911-1995)

[z] God: a disease we imagine we are cured of because no one dies of it nowadays.

[The Trouble with Being Born]

Arthur C. Clarke
(1917-2008)

[a] A faith that cannot survive collision with the truth is not worth many regrets.

[quoted from Ciaran Hanway,
Omnipurpose Page]

William Kingdon Clifford
(1845-1879)

[b] It is wrong always, everywhere and for everyone to believe anything upon insufficient evidence.

[The Ethics Of Belief]

[c] If a man, holding a belief which he was taught in childhood or persuaded of afterwards, keeps down and pushes away any doubts which arise about it in his mind, purposely avoids the reading of books and the company of men that call in question or discuss it... the life of that man is one long sin against mankind.

[Ibid.]

Chapman Cohen
(1868-1954)

[d] [T]he defenders of godism are now shrieking against the growing number of Atheists, and there is a call to the religious world to enter upon a crusade against Atheism. The stage in which heresy meant little more than all exchange of one god for another has passed. It has become a case of acceptance or rejection of the idea of God, and the growth is with

those who reject.

["Deity And Design"]

Edmund D. Cohen
(?-?)

[e] While the Bible does not explicitly say that independent thinking is a cardinal sin -- to do so would give the game away -- it is the crux of any biblically authentic definition of sin, one incompatible with doing the devotional program.

[The Mind of the Bible Believer]

[f] The content of the teaching, as well as the form of social relations, is set up so as to dig a psychological moat around the believers.

[Ibid.]

Nick Cohen
(?-   )

[g] Abraham's readiness to obey the order of a jealous, not to say psychopathic, God to "take now thy son, thine only son Isaac, whom thou lovest, and get thee into the land of Moriah; and offer him there for a burnt offering" is divine justification for murderous servility. A servant who will slaughter his son on the whim of the Lord will do anything.

[The Observer,
7 October 2001]

Sir Edward Coke
(1552-1634)

[h] The house of every one is to him his castle and fortress, as well for his defense against injury and violence as for his repose.
[Semayne's Case.
5 Rep. 91]

Lucy Colman
(1817-1906)

[i] I wish to be just to all, but the Christian church, with its religion, seems to me a blot

upon civilization.

[from The Truth Seeker Annual and Freethinkers' Almanac, 1889]

[j] Christianity demands entire subordination to its edicts, no matter that it keeps out of sight the damnation of infants in another world, if it subjugates all children to its decrees by teaching them, not only in Sunday-schools but in public schools supported by the public at large, the doctrines taught in the Bible. Until the majority of the people are emancipated from authority over their minds, we are not safe.

[Reminiscences]

Hans Conzelmann
(1915-1989)

[k] The Christian community continues to exist because the conclusions of the critical study of the Bible are largely withheld from them.

[unsourced]

William Cowper
(1731-1800)

[l] How sweet, how passing sweet, is solitude! But grant me still a friend in my retreat, whom I may whisper, Solitude is sweet.

[Retirement. Line 740]

Stephen Crane
(1871-1900)

[m] A man said to the universe:
"Sir, I exist!"
"However," replied the universe,
"That fact has not created in me a sense of obligation."

[War Is Kind. Fragment]

Michael Crichton
(1942-   )

[n] One of the defining features of religion is that your beliefs are not troubled by facts, because they have nothing to do with facts.

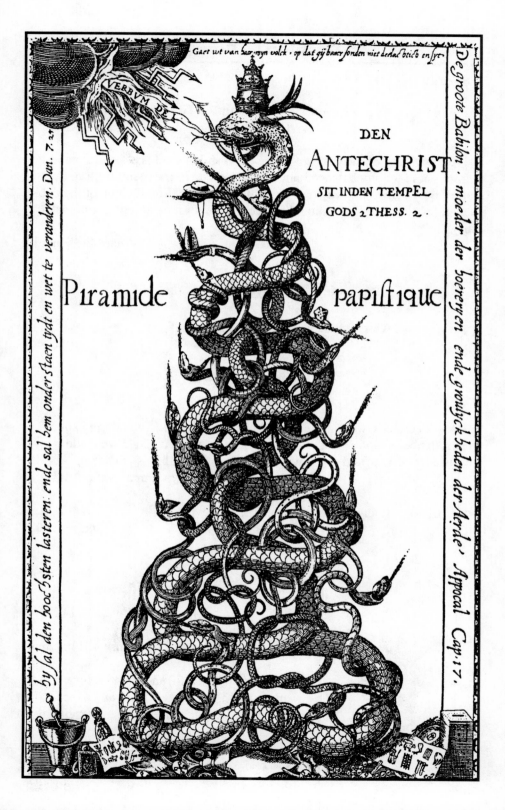

VERBVM DEI

Gaet wt van baex myn volck · op dat gij haer sonden niet deelac otich en syt

DEN
ANTECHRIST
SIT INDEN TEMPEL
GODS 2 THESS. 2 ·

Piramide

papistique

De groote Babilon · moeder der hoereryen ende grouwelyckheden der Aerde · Appocal Cap. 17 ·

by sal den hooch sten lasteren: ende sal hem onderstaen tyde en wet te veranderen. Dan. 7. 25

[remarks To The Commonwealth Club, 15 September 2003]

Francis Harry Compton Crick
(1916-2004)

[o] A knowledge of the true age of the earth and of the fossil record makes it impossible for any balanced intellect to believe in the literal truth of every part of the Bible in the way that fundamentalists do. And if some of the Bible is manifestly wrong, why should any of the rest of it be accepted automatically?

[What Mad Pursuit]

Critias
(480-403 B.C.E.)

[p] It was man who first made men believe in gods.

[unsourced]

David Cronenberg
(1943-   )

[q] And I certainly went through all those things as a kid wondering about the existence of God or not, but at a very early age, I decided we made it up because we were afraid and it was one way to make things palatable.

[Film Threat. February 1997]

[r] [I'm] not just an atheist, but a total nonbeliever.

[Esquire. 1992]

Aleister Crowley
(1875-1947)

[s] The Gods are but names for the forces of Nature themselves.

[Magick in Theory and Practice]

[t] I slept with Faith, and found a corpse in my arms on awaking; I drank and danced all night with Doubt, and found her a virgin in the morning.

[The Book Of Lies]

[u] If one were to take the Bible seriously one would go mad. But to take the Bible seriously, one must be already mad.

[unsourced]

Rauf Cudworth
(1617-1688)

[v] Because theists themselves acknowledge God to be incomprehensible, it may be from thence inferred that he is a nonentity.

[True Intellectual System of the Universe]

Ely Culbertson
(1891-1955)

[w] The bizarre world of cards... a world of pure power politics where rewards and punishments were meted out immediately. A deck of cards was built like the purest of hierarchies, with every card a master to those below it a lackey to those above it.

[Total Peace. Chap. 1]

Gabriele D'Annunzio
(1863-1938)

[x] Blessed are the youths who hunger and thirst for glory, for they shall be satisfied.

[unsourced]

[y] Everything in life depends upon the eternally new. Man must either renew himself or die.

[unsourced]

Clarence Darrow
(1857-1938)

[z] I don't believe in God because I don't believe in Mother Goose.

[speech, Toronto, 1930]

[a] To think is to differ.

[Scopes trial, July 1925]

[b] Ignorance and fanaticism are ever busy and need feeding. Always feeding and gloating for more. Today it is the public school teachers; tomorrow the private. The next day the preachers and the lecturers, the magazines, the books, the newspapers. After a while,

Your Honor, it is the setting of man against man and creed against creed until with flying banners and beating drums we are marching backward to the glorious ages of the sixteenth century when bigots lighted fagots to burn the men who dared to bring any intelligence and enlightenment and culture to the human mind.

[Scopes trial, 1925]

[c] I say that religion is the belief in future life and in God. I don't believe in either.

[interview, N.Y. Times, 19 April 1936]

[d] In spite of all the yearnings of men, no one can produce a single fact or reason to support the belief in God...

[The Sign, May 1938]

Charles Darwin
(1809-1882)

[e] Ignorance more frequently begets confidence than does knowledge: it is those who know little, and not those who know much, who so positively assert that this or that problem will never be solved by science.

[The Ascent of Man]

Sir Francis Dashwood
(1708-1781)

[f] Man has a natural right to be free... by Freedom is not nor can be meant that every individual should act as he lists, and according as he is swayed by his own Passions, Vices, or Infirmities: but freedom is a right every man has to do what he will with his own...

[as quoted in Hell-Fire Friars by Gerald Suster]

John Davidson
(1857-1909)

[g] Do I believe in Heaven and Hell? I do; we have them here; the world is nothing else.
[Dedication to the Generation Knocking at the Door]

Richard Dawkins
(1941-   )

[h] The survival value of the god meme in the meme pool results from its great psychological appeal. It provides a superficially plausible answer to deep and troubling questions about existence. It suggests that injustices in this world may be rectified in the next. The "everlasting arms" hold out a cushion against our own inadequacies which, like a doctor's placebo, is none the less effective for being imaginary.

[The Selfish Gene]

[i] Another meme of the religious meme complex is called faith. It means blind trust, in the absence of evidence, even in the teeth of evidence. The story of Doubting Thomas is told, not so that we shall admire Thomas, but so that we can admire the other apostles in comparison. Thomas demanded evidence. Nothing is more lethal for certain kinds of memes than a tendency to look for evidence. The other apostles, whose faith was so strong that they did not need evidence, are held up to us as worthy of imitation. The meme for blind faith secures its own perpetuation by the simple unconscious expedient of discouraging rational inquiry.

[Ibid.]

[j] Faith cannot move mountains (though generations of children are solemnly told the contrary and believe it). But it is capable of driving people to such dangerous folly that faith seems to me to qualify as a kind of mental illness. It leads people to believe in whatever it is so strongly that in extreme cases they are prepared to kill and to die for it without the need for further justification.

[Ibid.]

[k] Blind faith can justify anything. In a man believes in a different god, or even if he uses a different ritual for worshipping the same god, blind faith can decree that he should die - on the cross, at the stake, skewered on a Crusader's sword, shot in a Beirut street, or blown up in a bar in Belfast. Memes for blind faith have their own ruthless ways of propagating themselves. This is true of patriotic and political as well as religious blind faith.

[Ibid.]

[l] Science offers us an explanation of how complexity (the difficult) arose out of simplicity (the easy). The hypothesis of God offers no worthwhile explanation for anything, for it simply postulates what we are trying to explain. It postulates the difficult to explain, and leaves it at that. We cannot prove that there is no God, but we can safely conclude the He is very, very improbable indeed.

[from the New Humanist, the Journal of the
Rationalist Press Association,
Vol. 107, No 2]

[m] The universe we observe has precisely the properties we should expect if there is, at bottom, no design, no purpose, no evil and no good, nothing but blind pitiless indifference.

[River Out Of Eden]

[n] The creationists' fondness for "gaps" in the fossil record is a metaphor for their love of gaps in knowledge generally. Gaps, by default, are filled by God. You don't know how the nerve impulse works? Good! You don't understand how memories are laid down in the brain? Excellent! Is photosynthesis a bafflingly complex process? Wonderful! Please don't go to work on the problem, just give up, and appeal to God. Dear scientist, don't work on your mysteries. Bring us your mysteries for we can use them. Don't squander precious ignorance by researching it away. Ignorance is God's gift to Kansas.

[Creationism: God's Gift To The Ignorant,
The Times, 21 May 2005]

[o] Intelligent design is not an argument of the same character as these controversies. It is not a scientific argument at all, but a religious one. It might be worth discussing in a class on the history of ideas, in a philosophy class on popular logical fallacies, or in a comparative religion class on origin myths from around the world. But it no more belongs in a biology class than alchemy belongs in a chemistry class, phlogiston in a physics class or the stork theory in a sex education class. In those cases, the demand for equal time for "both theories" would be ludicrous. Similarly, in a class on 20th-century European history, who would demand equal time for the theory that the Holocaust never happened? ... If complex organisms demand an explanation, so does a complex designer. And it's no solution to raise the theologian's plea that God (or the Intelligent Designer) is simply immune to the normal demands of scientific explanation. To do so would be to shoot yourself in the foot. You cannot have it both ways. Either ID belongs in the science classroom, in which case it must submit to the discipline required of a scientific hypothesis. Or it does not, in which case get it out of the science classroom and send it back into the church, where it belongs.

[(co-author with Jerry Coyne) The Guardian, 1 September 2005]

[p] Faith is the great cop-out, the great excuse to evade the need to think and evaluate evidence. Faith is belief in spite of, even perhaps because of, the lack of evidence.

[unsourced]

Daniel Defoe
(1660-1731)

[q] Wherever God erects a house of prayer,
The Devil always builds a chapel there;
And 'twill be found, upon examination,
The latter has the largest congregation.

[The True-Born Englishman]

Daniel Dennett
(1942-   )

[r] The kindly God who lovingly fashioned each and every one of us and sprinkled the sky with shining stars for our delight -- that God is, like Santa Claus, a myth of childhood, not anything a sane, undeluded adult could literally believe in. That God must either be turned into a symbol for something less concrete or abandoned altogether.

[Darwin's Dangerous Idea]

[s] It is undeniable that astrology provides its adherents with a highly articulated system of patterns that they think they see in the events of the world. The difference, however, is that no one has ever been able to get rich by betting on the patterns, but only by selling the patterns to others.

[Brainchildren]

Mary Ainge De Vere
("Madeline Bridges")
(1844-1920)

[t] For life is the mirror of king and slave, 'tis just what we are and do.

[Life's Mirror.
Stanza 1]

King Diamond
(1956-   )

[u] We have these human instincts and if we don't go by them we won't survive. It's as simple as that. And those who are trying to tell people: "Hey, go by this book here and you'll be saved forever." ...god, you will not be saved! You'll be the easiest victim of all.

[interview from The Black Flame.
Vol. 4, #s 3 & 4]

Emily Dickinson
(1830-1886)

[v] The soul selects her own society, then shuts the door.

[Life. XIII, Exclusion,
Stanza 1]

[w] When we think of his lone effort to live and its bleak reward, the mind turns to the myth "for His mercy endureth forever," with confiding revulsion.

[to her cousins Louise and Frances Norcross]

[x] "Faith" is a fine invention, when gentlemen can see
But microscopes are prudent, in an emergency.

[Complete Poems,
1924]

[y] Those -- dying then,
Knew where they went --
They went to God' Right Hand --
That Hand is amputated now
And God cannot be found...

["Those -- dying then"]

Denis Diderot
(1713-1784)

[z] To attempt the destruction of our passions is the height of folly. What a noble aim is that of the zealot who tortures himself like a madman in order to desire nothing, love nothing, feel nothing, and who, if he succeeded, would end up a complete monster!

[Philosophic Thoughts, 1746]

[a] The Judaical and Christian theology show us a partial god who chooses or rejects, who loves or hates, according to his caprice; in short, a tyrant who plays with his creatures; who punishes in this world the whole human species for the crimes of a single man; who predestines the greater number of mortals to be his enemies, to the end that he may punish them to all eternity, for having received from him the liberty of declaring against him.

[footnote to d'Holbach's The System Of Nature]

[b] To prove the Gospels by a miracle is to prove an absurdity by something contrary to nature.

[unsourced]

[c] When God, from whom I have my reason, demands of me to sacrifice it, he becomes a mere juggler that snatches from me what he pretended to give.

[A Philosophical Conversation, 1777]

Marlene Dietrich
(1901-1992)

[d] If there is a supreme being, he's crazy.

[Rave, November 1986]

Diogenes Laertius
(ca. 200)

[e] Asked what he gained from philosophy, he answered, "To do without being commanded what others do from fear of the laws."

[Aristotle. 11]

[f] They say that the first inclination which an animal has is to protect itself.

[Zeno. 19]

Walt Disney
(1901-1966)

[g] If I were a fatalist, or a mystic, which I decidedly am not, it might be appropriate to say I believe in my lucky star. But I reject "luck" -- I feel every person creates his own "determinism" by discovering his best aptitudes and following them undeviatingly.

[Wisdom Magazine.
Vol. 32, December 1959]

[h] Our schools should put more emphasis on how to go about finding out.

[Ibid.]

Benjamin Disraeli,
Earl of Beaconsfield
(1804-1881)

[i] The secret of success is consistency to purpose.

[Address, House of Commons.
1 May 1865]

[j] Little things affect little minds.

[Sybil. Book III, Chap. 11]

Henry Austin Dobson
(1840-1921)

[k] Time goes, you say? Ah no! Alas, Time stays, we go.

[The Paradox of Time. Stanza 1]

Samuel Dodge
(Floruit 1868)

[l] You may go through this world, but 'twill be very slow if you listen to all that is said as you go; You'll be worried and fretted and kept in a stew, for meddlesome tongues must have

something to do, for people will talk, you know.

[People Will Talk. Stanza 1]

John Donne
(1573-1631)

[m] The snail, which everywhere doth roam carrying his own house still, still is at home,
Follow (for he is easy paced) this snail,
Be thine own palace, or the world's thy jail.

[Verse Letter to Sir Henry Wotton]

Fyodor Dostoyevsky
(1821-1881)

[n] This craving for community of worship is the chief misery of every man individually and of all humanity from the beginning of time. For the sake of common worship, they've slain each other with the sword. They have set up gods and challenged each other, "Put away your gods and come and worship ours, or we will kill you and your gods!"

[The Brothers Karamazov]

George Norman Douglas
(1868-1952)

[o] I can find no room in my cosmos for a deity save as a waste product of human weakness, the excrement of the imagination.

[South Wind. 1917]

Frederick Douglass
(1818-1895)

[p] My long-crushed spirit rose, cowardice departed, bold defiance took its place; and I resolved that, however long I might remain a slave in form, the day had passed forever when I could be a slave in fact.

[Narrative of the Life of
Frederick Douglass,
an American Slave]

John William Draper
(1811-1882)

[q] We must bear in mind that the majority of men are imperfectly educated, and hence we must not needlessly offend the religious ideas of our age. It is enough for us ourselves to know that, though there is a Supreme Power, there is no Supreme Being. There is an invisible principle, but not a personal God, to whom it would be not so much blasphemy as absurdity to impute the form, the sentiments, the passions of man. All revelation is, necessarily, a mere fiction. That which men call chance is only the effect of an unknown cause. Even of chances there is a law. There is no such thing as Providence, for Nature proceeds under irresistible laws, and in this respect the universe is only a vast automatic engine. The vital force which pervades the world is what the illiterate call God. The modifications through which all things are running take place in an irresistible way, and hence it may be said that the progress of the world is, under Destiny, like a seed, it can evolve only in a predetermined mode.

[History Of The Conflict Between
Religion And Science]

Theodore Dreiser
(1871-1945)

[r] Assure a man that he has a soul and then frighten him with old wives' tales as to what is to become of him afterward, and you have hooked a fish, a mental slave.

[unsourced]

W. E. B. DuBois
(1868-1963)

[s] I think the greatest gift of the Soviet Union to modern civilization was the dethronement of the clergy and the refusal to let religion be taught in the public schools.
[The Autobiography of W. E. B. DuBois]

John Dryden
(1631-1700)

[t] Of ancient race by birth, but nobler yet in

his own worth.

[Absalom and Achitophel. Part I, Line 900]

[u] Beware the fury of a patient man.

[Ibid. Line 1005]

[v] Genius must be born, and never can be taught.

[Epistle to Congreve. Line 60]

Edward Dyer
(ca. 1540-1607)

[w] My mind to me a kingdom is;
Such present joys therein I find,
That it excels all other bliss that the earth affords or grows by kind.

[MS. Rawl. 85, p. 17]

**Thomas Alva Edison
(1847-1931)**

[x] I have never seen the slightest scientific proof of the religious theories of heaven and hell, of future life for individuals, or of a personal God.

[from Columbian Magazine]

[y] All Bibles are man-made.

[unsourced]

[z] The great trouble is that the preachers get the children from six to seven years of age, and then it is almost impossible to do anything with them. Incurably religious -- that is the best way to describe the mental condition of so many people. Incurably religious.

[quoted by Joseph Lewis from a personal conversation]

**Greg Egan
(1961-   )**

[a] Most Christian theologians have retreated from all the things that their religion supposedly asserts; they take a much more "modern" view than the average believer. But by the time you've "modernized" something like Christianity -- starting off with "Genesis was all just poetry" and ending up with "Well,

of course there's no such thing as a personal God" -- there's not much point pretending that there's anything religious left.

[interview published in Eidolon, 11 January 1993]

Barbara Ehrenreich
(1941-   )

[b] If we are responsible for our actions, as most religions insist, then God should be, too, and I would propose an immediate withdrawal of prayer and other forms of flattery... at least until an apology is issued.

["God Owes Us an Apology"]

Paul R. Ehrlich
(1932-   )

[c] I have understood the population explosion intellectually for a long time. I came to understand it emotionally one stinking hot night in Delhi a couple years ago. My wife and daughter and I were returning to our hotel in an ancient taxi. The seats were hopping with fleas. As we crawled through the city, we entered a crowded slum area. The temperature was well over 100, and the air was a haze of dust and smoke. The streets seemed alive with people. People eating, people washing, people sleeping. People visiting, arguing and screaming. People thrusting their hands, begging. People defecating and urinating. People clinging to buses. People herding animals. People, people, people, people.

[The Population Bomb]

Albert Einstein
(1879-1955)

[d] It was, of course, a lie what you read about my religious convictions, a lie which is being systematically repeated. I do not believe in a personal God and I have never denied this but have expressed it clearly. If something is in me which can be called religious then it is the unbounded admiration for the structure of the world so far as our science can reveal it.

[Albert Einstein: The Human Side]

[e] The idea of a personal God is an anthropo-

logical concept which I am unable to take seriously.

[letter to Hoffman and Dukas, 1946]

[f] The man who is thoroughly convinced of the universal operation of the law of causation cannot for a moment entertain the idea of a being who interferes in the course of events... He has no use for the religion of fear and equally little for social or moral religion.

[Ideas and Opinions]

[g] The most beautiful experience we can have is the mysterious. It is the fundamental emotion which stands at the cradle of true art and true science. Whoever does not know it and can no longer wonder, no longer marvel, is as good as dead, and his eyes are dimmed.

[The World As I See It]

George Eliot
(1819-1880)

[h] Your dunce who can't do his sums always has a taste for the infinite.

["Felix Holt, the Radical," 1860]

[i] Where is that Goshen of mediocrity in which a smattering of science and learning will pass for profound instruction, where platitudes will be accepted as wisdom, bigoted narrowness as holy zeal, unctuous egoism as God-given piety? Let such a man become an evangelical preacher; he will then find it possible to reconcile small ability with great ambition, superficial knowledge with the prestige of erudition, a middling morale with a high reputation for sanctity.

["Evangelical Teaching"]

Havelock Ellis
(1859-1939)

[j] And it is in his own image, let us remember, that Man creates God.

[unsourced]

[k] The omnipresent process of sex, as it is woven into the whole texture of our man's or woman's body, is the pattern of all process of

our life.

[The New Spirit]

[l] That indeed were a world fit to perish, wherein the moralist had set up the ignoble maxim: Safety first.

[Little Essays of Love and Virtue.
Chap. 2]

[m] What we call "morals" is simply blind obedience to words of command.

[The Dance of Life. Chap. 6]

[n] The eugenic ideal which is now developing is not an artificial product, but the reasoned manifestation of a natural instinct, which has often been far more severely strained by the arbitrary prohibitions of the past than it is ever likely to be by any eugenic ideals of the future.

[The Task of Social Hygiene]

Ralph Waldo Emerson
(1803-1882)

[o] We must get rid of that Christ, we must get rid of that Christ!

[from John E. Remsberg, The Christ, 1909]

[p] As men's prayers are a disease of the will, so are their creeds a disease of the intellect.

[Self-Reliance]

[q] An actually existent fly is more important than a possibly existent angel.

[unsourced]

[r] Leave this hypocritical prating about the masses. Masses are rude, lame, unmade, pernicious in their demands and influence, and need not to be flattered, but to be schooled. I wish not to concede anything to them, but to tame, drill, divide, and break them up, and draw individuals out of them.

[Considerations By The Way,
The Conduct Of Life]

[s] He is great who is what he is from Nature,

ℭThe parlyament of deuylles.

AS Mary was grette with Gabryell
And had concepued and borne a chylde
All þ deuylles of the erthe of þ ayre & of hell
Helde theyr parlyament of þ mayde mylde
ℭwhat man had mad her wombe to swel
ℭo tempt her þe tende to sylde
Her chyldes fader who can tell
who dyde with her tho werkes wylde

and who never reminds us of others.

[Representative Men.
Uses of Great Men]

[t] One of the benefits of a college education is to show the boy its little avail.

[Conduct of Life. Culture.]

[u] Next to the originator of a good sentence is the first quoter of it.

[Quotation and Originality]

[v] Let me never fall into the vulgar mistake of dreaming that I am persecuted whenever I am contradicted.

[Journals, 1838]

Quintus Ennius
(239-169 B.C.E.)

[w] No sooner said than done -- so acts your man of worth.

[Annals. Book 9]

Epicurus
(341-271 B.C.E.)

[x] I have never wished to cater to the crowd; for what I know they do not approve, and what they approve I do not know.

[Fragments]

[y] Is God willing to prevent evil, but not able? Then he is not omnipotent. Is he able, but not willing? Then he is malevolent. Is he both able and willing? Then whence cometh evil? Is he neither able nor willing? Then why call him God?

[unsourced]

[z] If the gods listened to the prayers of men, all humankind would quickly perish since they constantly pray for many evils to befall one another.

[quoted from Eugene O'Connor,
The Essential Epicurus]

Euripides
(ca. 480-406 B.C.E.)

[a] Do we, holding that the gods exist, deceive ourselves with insubstantial dreams and lies, while random careless chance and change alone control the world?

[Hecuba]

[b] I sacrifice to no god save myself -- And to my belly, greatest of deities.

[The Cyclops]

Julius Evola
(1898-1974)

[c] What I am about to say does not concern the ordinary man of our day. On the contrary, I have in mind the man who finds himself involved in today's world, even at its most problematic and paroxysmal points; yet he does not belong inwardly to such a world, nor will he give in to it. He feels himself, in essence, as belonging to a different race from that of the overwhelming majority of his contemporaries.

[Ride The Tiger]

Jerry Falwell
(1933-2007)

[d] Christians, like slaves and soldiers, ask no questions.

[unsourced]

Jules Feiffer
(1929-   )

[e] Christ died for our sins. Dare we make his martyrdom meaningless by not committing them?

[unsourced]

Ludwig Andreas Feuerbach
(1804-1872)

[f] Whenever morality is based on theology, whenever right is made dependent on divine authority, the most immoral, unjust, infamous things can be justified and established.

[The Essence Of Christianity]

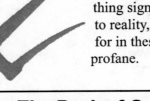

[g] The present age ... prefers the sign to the thing signified, the copy to the original, fancy to reality, the appearance to the essence ... for in these days illusion only is sacred, truth profane.

[Ibid. Preface]

[h] Christianity has in fact long vanished, not only from the reason but also from the life of mankind, and it is nothing more than a fixed idea.

[On Philosophy and Christianity]

[i] It is clear as the sun and as evident as the day that there is no God, and still more that there can be none.

[unsourced]

Henry Fielding
(1707-1754)

[j] There are a set of religions, or rather moral writings, which teach that virtue is the certain road to happiness, and vice to misery, in this world. A very wholesome and comfortable doctrine, and to which we have but one objection, namely, that it is not true.

[unsourced]

W.C. Fields
(1880-1946)

[k] Prayers never bring anything... They may bring solace to the sap, the bigot, the ignorant, the aboriginal, and the lazy -- but to the enlightened it is the same as asking Santa Claus to bring you something for Christmas.

[unsourced]

Millard Fillmore
(1800-1874)

[l] ...if any sect suffered itself to be used for political objects I would meet it by political opposition. In my view church and state should be separate, not only in form, but fact.

[address during 1856 Presidential election]

John Fiske
(1842-1901)

[m] Is it honest for me to go and sit there on communion day and drink the wine and eat the bread while feeling it all to be mummery?

[letter to his mother, 20 March 1860]

Gustave Flaubert
(1821-1880)

[n] I hate the crowd, the herd. It seems to me always atrociously stupid and vile... The sight of their vulgarities and of their very hats and overcoats, the things they said and the sound of their voices made me feel like vomiting and weeping all at once. Never since I have been in this world have I felt so suffocated by a disgust for mankind.

[letter to his mother]

Antony Flew
(1923-   )

[o] If it is to be established that there is a God, then we have to have good grounds for believing that this is indeed so. Until and unless some such grounds are produced we have literally no reason at all for believing; and in that situation the only reasonable posture must be that of either the negative atheist or the agnostic. So the onus of proof has to rest on the proposition.

[The Presumption Of Atheism]

[p] You cannot ... transmute some incoherent mixture of words into sense merely by introducing the three-letter word "God" to be its grammatical subject.

[How to Think Straight]

George William Foote
(1850-1915)

[q] Atheists are often charged with blasphemy, but it is a crime they cannot commit ... When the Atheist examines, denounces, or satirizes the gods, he is not dealing with persons but with ideas. He is incapable of insulting God, for he does not admit the existence of any such being... We attack not a person but a belief, not a being but an idea, not a fact but a fancy.

[Flowers Of Freethought]

Anatole France
(1844-1924)

[r] People who have no weaknesses are ter-

rible; there is no way of taking advantage of them.

[The Crime of Sylvestre Bonnard. The Log,
24 December 1849. Part II, Chap.4]

[s] The faculty of doubting is rare among men. A few choice spirits carry the germ of it in them, but these do not develop without training.

[Penguin Island. Book VI, Chap. 2]

[t] The average man, who does not know what to do with his life, wants another one which will last forever.

[unsourced]

[u] Nature has no [moral] principles... makes no distinction between good and evil.

[unsourced]

Benjamin Franklin
(1706-1790)

[v] Those who would give up essential Liberty, to purchase a little temporary Safety, deserve neither Liberty nor Safety.

[reply to the Pennsylvania Assembly
to the governor, 11 November 1755]

[w] Lighthouses are more helpful than churches.

[Poor Richard's Almanack. 1758]

[x] The way to see by faith is to shut the eye of reason.

[Ibid.]

[y] I have found Christian dogma unintelligible. Early in life I absented myself from Christian assemblies.

[Toward The Mystery]

Nat Freedland
(?-?)

[z] [Anton LaVey] believes in an ordered society that can protect its inhabitants against crime, is totally against drugs as a magic tool,

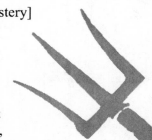

and remains unsympathetic to the hippie ethos because of its denial of the ego... He was thoroughly offended by the sudden plague of supposedly Devil-inspired [Manson Family] murders in California, calling the bootleg Satanists "kooks and creeps out of their mind on drugs."

[The Occult Explosion]

Sigmund Freud
(1856-1939)

[a] Neither in my private life nor in my writings, have I ever made a secret of being an out-and-out unbeliever.

[letter to Charles Singer]

[b] Religious ideas have sprung from the same need as all the other achievements of culture: from the necessity for defending itself against the crushing supremacy of nature.

[The Future of an Illusion. 1927]

[c] Devout believers are safeguarded in a high degree against the risk of certain neurotic illnesses; their acceptance of the universal neurosis spares them the task of constructing the personal one.

[Ibid.]

[d] When a man has once brought himself to accept uncritically all the absurdities that religious doctrines put before him and even to overlook the contradictions between them, we need not be greatly surprised at the weakness of his intellect.

[Ibid.]

[e] If the sole reason why you must not kill your neighbor is because God has forbidden it and will severely punish you for it in this or the next life -- then, when you learn that there is no God and that you need not fear His punishment, you will certainly kill your neighbor without hesitation, and you can only be prevented from doing so by mundane force. Thus either these dangerous masses must be held down most severely and kept most carefully away from any chance of intellectual awakening, or else the relationship

between civilization and religion must undergo a fundamental revision.
[Ibid.]

[f] Demons do not exist any more than gods do, being only the products of the psychic activity of man.
[from New York Times Magazine, 6 May 1956]

[g] Most people do not really want freedom, because freedom involves responsibility, and most people are frightened of responsibility.
[Civilization and Its Discontents]

[h] In the long run, nothing can withstand reason and experience, and the contradiction religion offers to both is palpable.
[unsourced]

Erich Fromm
(1900-1980)

[i] The majority of men have not yet acquired the maturity to be independent, to be rational, to be objective. They need myths and idols to endure the fact that man is all by himself, that there is no authority which gives meaning to life except man himself.
[Escape From Freedom.
Foreword II]

[j] Once a doctrine, however irrational, has gained power in a society, millions of people will believe it rather than feel ostracized and isolated.
[An Analysis Of Some Types Of Religious Experience]

[k] If faith cannot be reconciled with rational thinking, it has to be eliminated as an anachronistic remnant of earlier stages of culture and replaced by science dealing with facts and theories which are intelligible and can be validated.
[Man For Himself, 1947]

[l] There is perhaps no phenomenon which contains so much destructive feeling as "moral indignation," which permits envy or hate to be acted out under the guise of virtue.
[Ibid.]

Robert Frost
(1874-1963)

[m] The best things and best people rise out of their separateness. I'm against a homogenized society because I want the cream to rise.

[unsourced]

Northrop Frye
(1912-1991)

[n] The metaphor of the king as the shepherd of his people goes back to ancient Egypt. Perhaps the use of this particular convention is due to the fact that, being stupid, affectionate, gregarious, and easily stampeded, the societies formed by sheep are most like human ones.

[Anatomy Of Criticism]

Robert W. Funk
(1926-2005)

[o] If the evidence supports the historical accuracy of the gospels, where is the need for faith? And if the historical reliability of the gospels is so obvious, why have so many scholars failed to appreciate the incontestable nature of the evidence?

[Honest to Jesus]

Matilda Joslyn Gage
(1826-1898)

[p] The careful student of history will discover that Christianity has been of very little value in advancing civilization, but has done a great deal toward retarding it.

[Woman, Church And State]

John Kenneth Galbraith
(1908-   )

[q] Had the Bible been in clear straightforward language, had the ambiguities and contradictions been edited out, and had the language been constantly modernized to accord with contemporary taste it would almost certainly have been, or become, a work of lesser influence.

[Economics, Peace and Laughter]

Galileo Galilei
(1564-1642)

[r] It is surely harmful to souls to make it a heresy to believe what is proved.
[The Authority of Scripture in Philosophical Controversies]

[s] I think that in the discussion of natural

problems we ought to begin not with the Scriptures, but with experiments, and demonstrations.

[Ibid.]

[t] To command the professors of astronomy to confute their own observations is to enjoin an impossibility, for it is to command them not to see what they do see, and not to understand what they do understand, and to find what they do not discover.

[Ibid.]

[u] They know that it is human nature to take up causes whereby a man may oppress his neighbor, no matter how unjustly... Hence they have had no trouble in finding men who would preach the damnability and heresy of the new doctrine from the very pulpit...

[1615]

Sir Francis Galton
(1822-1911)

[v] Our human civilized stock is far more weakly through congenital imperfection than that of any other species of animals, whether wild or domestic... If a twentieth part of the cost and pains were spent in measures for the improvement of the human race that is spent on the improvement of the breed of horses and cattle, what a galaxy of genius might we not create.

[Hereditary Talent and Character]

Helen H. Gardener
(1853-1925)

[w] Every injustice that has ever been fastened upon women in a Christian country has been "authorized by the Bible" and riveted and perpetuated by the pulpit.

[Men, Women And Gods]

[x] This religion and the Bible require of woman everything, and give her nothing. They ask her support and her love, and repay her with contempt and oppression.

[Ibid.]

William H. Gates
(1955-   )

[y] Just in terms of allocation of time resources, religion is not very efficient. There's a lot more I could be doing on a Sunday morning.

[TIME. 13 January 1996]

Théophile Gautier
(1811-1872)

[z] Virginity, mysticism, melancholy! Three unknown words, three new maladies brought by Christ.

[unsourced]

Edward Gibbon
(1737-1794)

[a] The winds and waves are always on the side of the ablest navigators.

[Decline and Fall
of the Roman Empire]

[b] To the philosophical eye the vices of the clergy are far less dangerous than their virtues.

[Ibid.]

[c] The theologian may indulge the pleasing task of describing Religion as she descended from Heaven, arrayed in her natural purity. A more melancholy duty is imposed on the historian. He must discover the inevitable mixture of error and corruption which she contracted in a long residence upon earth, among a weak and degenerate race of beings.

[Ibid.]

André Paul Guillaume Gide
(1869-1951)

[d] What another would have done as well as you, do not do it. What another would have said as well as you, do not say it; written as well, do not write it. Be faithful to that which exists nowhere but in yourself -- and thus make

yourself indispensable.

[Les Nourritures Terrestres. Envoi]

[e] A unanimous chorus of praise is not an assurance of survival; authors who please everyone at once are quickly exhausted.

[Pretexts]

[f] Christianity, above all, consoles; but there are naturally happy souls who do not need consolation. Consequently, Christianity begins by making such souls unhappy, for otherwise it would have no power over them.

[journal entry, 10 October 1893]

H. R. Giger
(1940-   )

[g] Since I have taken the path of art, it is like a kind of LSD trip - with no return. I feel like a tightrope walker; I see no difference between work and free time. Suddenly, I became aware that art is a vital activity that keeps me from falling into madness.

[quote, 1984]

Charlotte Perkins Gilman
(1860-1935)

[h] The stony-minded orthodox were right in fearing the first movement of new knowledge and free thought. It has gone on, and will go on, irresistibly, until some day we shall have no respect for an alleged "truth" which cannot stand the full blaze of knowledge, the full force of active thought.

[The Living of Charlotte Perkins Gilman]

Peter H. Gilmore
(1958-   )

[i] Each person is endowed with a different level of raw talent and thus some people are intrinsically worth more than others. No men are born equal!

["Stratification: A Hard Reality"
from The Black Flame.
Vol. 3, #3 and #4]

[j] [Richard] Strauss actively rejected Christianity and its disgusting creed of self-sacrifice. He saw life as a heroic struggle and himself as his own god. Thus when he composed a tone poem called "A Hero's Life," one should not be surprised that he Satanically made it a self-portrait. In this, he depicts himself as a mighty life-embracing warrior, who enjoys the battle against his critics -- lampooned as the toads they were, and who enjoyed his sensuous pleasures as well.

["Richard Strauss: Helden-Composer" from
The Black Flame. Vol. 3, #3 and #4]

[k] Behold the utter desperation of Christianity in its last gasp to find an enemy which can frighten the gullible into their churches. This enemy is but a projection of their own misdeeds which stem from the heart of their anti-life creed. Let them feed on themselves, as followers of the flaccid Nazarene should.

["The Tide Turns" from The Black Flame. Vol. 4, #3 and #4]

[l] We must cultivate a neo-Darwinian arena wherein opinions may clash in the bright glare of mid-day, light glinting off sabre-sharp tongues which slash against the armor of cultivated wit and erudition in a true conflict of rip-roaring repartée. We expect to see the sands stained crimson and will be ready to wield our discrimination boldly, without stint, to either raise a thumb in approval or give the sign of rejection.

["Pervasive Pantywaistism"
from The Black Flame. Vol. 6, #s 1 & 2]

[m] Satanists are not seeking saviors, which is why we have opted out of the majority of doctrines offered by the rest of the world's religions. We look with particular contempt on those who approach us, offering their (always unproven) "talents" towards advancing Satanism from what they, as outsiders, perceive as stasis. If they only knew. But they can't, and they will move on to those who cry out for direction -- lemmings have never been in short supply, whether they wear crosses or pentagrams.

["Towards The Well-Known Religion"
from The Black Flame. Vol. 6, #s 3 & 4]

[n] It is up to each member [of the Church of Satan] to apply Satanism and determine what political means will reach his/her ends, and they are each solely responsible for this decision. Freedom and responsibility -- must be a novel concept for those who aren't Satanists. We take it in stride.

["A Map for the Misdirected"
from Not Like Most. Issue 10]

[o] We don't accept faith or mysticism. We demand bedrock knowledge -- Understanding -- which can come from outward research and observation as well as carnal intuition. We also acknowledge that people have varied abilities to grasp such knowledge... you either have the talent to see these things or you do not -- it is not a matter of effort, but nature.

[Ibid.]

George Gissing
(1857-1903)

[p] It is because nations tend to stupidity and baseness that mankind moves so slowly; it is because individuals have a capacity for better things that it moves at all.

[The Private Papers of Henry Ryecroft. I, 16]

[q] Education is a thing of which only the few are capable; teach as you will only a small percentage will profit by your most zealous energy.

[Ibid. 22]

Josiah William Gitt
(1884-1973)

[r] Humanity's most valuable assets have been the non-conformists. Were it not for the non-conformists, he who refuses to be satisfied to go along with the continuance of things as they are, and insists upon attempting to find new ways of bettering things, the world would have know little progress, indeed.

[Gazette and Daily,
2 February 1957]

Paul Joseph Goebbels
(1897-1945)

[s] We have made the Reich by propaganda.
[Address at Essen,
25 June 1939]

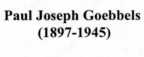

Johann Wolfgang von Goethe
(1749-1832)

[t] None is of freedom or of life-deserving unless he daily conquers it anew.

[Faust, Part Two]

[u] Rest not! Life is sweeping by; go and dare before you die. Something mighty and sublime, leave behind to conquer time.

[unsourced]

[v] Nature! We are surrounded and embraced by her: powerless to separate ourselves from her, and powerless to penetrate beyond her
Without asking, or warning, she snatches us up into her circling dance, and whirls us on until we are tired, and drop from her arms.

[Huxley]

[w] There is nothing more terrifying than ignorance in action.

[engraved on a plaque at the Naval War College]

Emma Goldman
(1869-1940)

[x] Christ and his teachings are the embodiment of submission, of inertia, of the denial of life; hence responsible for the things done in their name.

["The Failure of Christianity." Mother Earth, April 1913]

[y] Christianity is most admirably adapted to the training of slaves, to the perpetuation of a slave society; in short, to the very conditions confronting us to-day. Indeed, never could society have degenerated to its present appalling stage, if not for the assistance of Christianity. The rulers of the earth have realized long ago what potent poison inheres in the Christian religion. That is the reason they foster it; that is why they leave nothing undone to instill it into the blood of the people. They know only too well that the subtleness of the Christian teachings is a more powerful protection against rebellion and discontent than the club or the gun.

[Ibid.]

[z] Everywhere and always, since its very

inception, Christianity has turned the earth into a vale of tears; always it has made of life a weak, diseased thing, always it has instilled fear in man, turning him into a dual being, whose life energies are spent in the struggle between body and soul. In decrying the body as something evil, the flesh as the tempter to everything that is sinful, man has mutilated his being in the vain attempt to keep his soul pure, while his body rotted away from the injuries and tortures inflicted upon it. The Christian religion and morality extols the glory of the Hereafter, and therefore remains indifferent to the horrors of the earth. Indeed, the idea of self-denial and of all that makes for pain and sorrow is its test of human worth, its passport to the entry into heaven.

[Ibid.]

[a] It is characteristic of theistic "tolerance" that no one really cares what the people believe in, just so they believe or pretend to believe.

[The Philosophy of Atheism]

[b] I do not believe in God, because I believe in man. Whatever his mistakes, man has for thousands of years past been working to undo the botched job your God has made.

[speaking from a pulpit in Detroit, 1898]

Stephen Jay Gould
(1941-2002)

[c] The fundamentalists, by knowing the answers before they start, and then forcing nature into the straitjacket of their discredited preconceptions, lie outside the domain of science – or of any honest intellectual inquiry.

[Bully for Brontosaurus]

[d] The argument that the literal story of Genesis can qualify as science collapses on three major grounds: the creationists' need to invoke miracles in order to compress the events of the earth's history into the biblical span of a few thousand years; their unwillingness to abandon claims clearly disproved, including the assertion that all fossils are products of Noah's flood; and their reliance upon distortion, misquote, half-quote, and citation out of context to characterise the ideas of their opponents.

[The Skeptical Inquirer, Winter 1987]

[e] Well, evolution is a theory. It is also a fact. And facts and theories are different things, not rungs in a hierarchy of increasing certainty. Facts are the world's data. Theories are structures of ideas that explain and interpret facts. Facts don't go away when scientists debate rival theories to explain them. Einstein's theory of gravitation replaced Newton's in this century, but apples didn't suspend themselves in midair, pending the outcome. And humans evolved from ape-like ancestors whether they did so by Darwin's proposed mechanism or by some other yet to be discovered.

[Science and Creationism, 1984]

[f] When people learn no tools of judgment and merely follow their hopes, the seeds of political manipulation are sown.

[quoted from About.com]

**Remy de Gourmont
(1858-1915)**

[g] I do not believe it useful to generalize opinions, to teach admirations. It is for each man to procure himself the emotion he needs, and the morality which suits him.

[Decadence]

**Madison Grant
(1865-1937)**

[h] True aristocracy is governed by the wisest and best, always a small minority in any population. Human society is like a serpent dragging its long body on the ground, but with the head always thrust a little in advance and a little elevated above the earth. The serpent's tail, in human society represented by the antisocial forces, was in the past dragged by sheer force along the path of progress. Such has been the organization of mankind from the beginning, and such it still is in older communities than ours. What progress humanity can make under the control of universal suffrage, or the rule of the average, may find a further analogy in the habits of certain snakes which wiggle sideways and disregard the head with its brain and eyes. Such serpents, however, are not noted for their ability to make rapid progress.

[The Passing of the Great Race]

Ulysses S. Grant
(1822-1885)

[i] Leave the matter of religion to the family altar, the church, and the private school, supported entirely by private contributions. Keep the church and the State forever separate.

[Speech at Des Moines, Iowa, 1875]

Ruth Hurmence Green
(1915-1981)

[j] Suppose you had never heard of Christianity, and that next Sunday morning a stranger standing in a pulpit told you about a book whose authors could not be authenticated and whose contents, written hundreds of years ago, included blood-curdling legends of slaughter and intrigue and fables about unnatural happenings such as virgin births, devils that inhabit bodies and talk, people rising from the dead and ascending live into the clouds, and suns that stand still. Suppose he then asked you to believe that an uneducated man described in that book was a god who could get you into an eternal fantasy-place called heaven, when you die. Would you as an intelligent, rational person even bother to read such nonsense, let alone pattern your entire life upon it?

[The Born Again Skeptic's Guide to the Bible]

[k] To preserve a guess born of imagination and fantasy in the Holy Book of Christianity, presenting it as the revealed Word of God, all to be taken on faith, is an insult to the intelligence and reasoning ability of members of societies which might be expected to have undergone some scientific advancement over a period of several thousand years, and comprises just one of the many absurd impositions of the Bible.

[Ibid.]

[l] I am now convinced that children should not be subjected to the frightfulness of the Christian religion... If the concept of a father who plots to have his own son put to death is presented to children as beautiful and as worthy of society's admiration, what types of

human behavior can be presented to them as reprehensible?

[Ibid. Preface]

[m] It is possible to pull out justification for imposing your will on others, simply by calling your will God's will.

[The Book of Ruth]

Robert Greene
(1959-   )

[n] To some people the notion of consciously playing power games -- no matter how indirect -- seems evil, asocial, a relic of the past. They believe they can opt out of the game by behaving in ways that have nothing to do with power. You must beware of such people, for while they express such opinions outwardly, they are often among the most adept players at power.

[The 48 Laws of Power]

[o] Striking imagery and grand symbolic gestures create the aura of power -- everyone responds to them. Stage spectacles for those around you, then, full of arresting visuals and radiant symbols that heighten your presence. Dazzled by appearances, no one will notice what you are really doing.

[Ibid.]

[p] Do not accept the roles that society foists on you. Re-create yourself by forging a new identity, one that commands attention and never bores the audience. Be the master of your own image rather than letting others define it for you.

[Ibid.]

[q] There are many different kinds of people in the world, and you can never assume that everyone will react to your strategies in the same way. Deceive or outmaneuver some people and they will spend the rest of their lives seeking revenge. They are wolves in lambs' clothing. Choose your victims and opponents carefully, then -- never offend or deceive the wrong person.

[Ibid.]

[r] You can die from someone else's misery -- emotional states are as infectious as diseases. You may feel you are helping the drowning man but you are only precipitating your own disaster. The unfortunate sometimes draw misfortune on themselves; they will also draw it on you.

[Ibid.]

Alfred Whitney Griswold
(1906-1963)

[s] In the long run of history, the censor and the inquisitor have always lost. The only sure weapon against bad ideas is better ideas. The source of better ideas is wisdom. The surest path to wisdom is a liberal education.

[Essays On Education]

Che Guevara
(1928-1967)

[t] In fact, if Christ himself stood in my way, I, like Nietzsche, would not hesitate to squish him like a worm.

[unsourced]

Arthur Guiterman
(1871-1943)

[u] Amoebas at the start were not complex;
They tore themselves apart and started Sex.

[Sex. Stanza 1]

E. Haldeman-Julius
(1889-1951)

[v] ...the Bible was a collection of books written at different times by different men -- a strange mixture of diverse human documents -- and a tissue of irreconcilable notions. Inspired? The Bible is not even intelligent. It is not even good craftsmanship, but is full of absurdities and contradictions.

[The Meaning Of Atheism]

[w] Don't take our word for it. Read the Bible itself. Read the statements of preachers. And you will understand that God is the most desperate character, the worst villain in all fiction.

[Ibid.]

[x] Christian theology has taught men that they should submit with unintelligent resignation to the worst real evils of life and waste their time in consideration of imaginary evils in "the life to come."

[Ibid.]

[y] A God of love, a God of wrath, a God of jealousy, a God of bigotry, a God of vulgar tirades, a God of cheating and lying -- yes, the Christian God is given all of these characteristics, and isn't it a wretched mess to be offered to men in this twentieth century? The beginning of wisdom, the beginning of humanism, the beginning of progress is the rejection of this

absurd, extravagantly impossible myth of a God.

[Ibid.]

[z] Remember that millions of Christians still base their belief in a God upon the words of the Bible, which is a collection of the most flabbergasting fictions ever imagined -- by men, too, who had lawless but very poor and crude imagination. Ingersoll and numerous other critics have shot the Christian holy book full of holes. It is worthless and proves nothing concerning the existence of a God. The idea of a God is worthless and unprovable.

[Ibid.]

[a] Why should an atheist pay more taxes so that a church which he despises should pay no taxes? That's a fair question. How can the apologists for the church exemption answer it?

["The Church Is a Burden, Not a Benefit, In Social Life"]

Thomas Hardy
(1840-1928)

[b] That faiths by which my comrades stand seem fantasies to me, and mirage-mist their Shining Land, is a strange destiny.

[The Impercipient at a Cathedral Service. Stanza 1]

Sam Harris
(1967-   )

[c] The only reason anyone is "moderate" in matters of faith these days is that he has assimilated some of the fruits of the last two thousand years of human thought... The doors leading out of scriptural literalism do not open from the inside. The moderation we see among nonfundamentalists is not some sign that faith itself has evolved; it is, rather, the product of the many hammer blows of modernity that have exposed certain tenets of faith to doubt.

[The End of Faith]

[d] Jesus Christ -- who, as it turns out, was born of a virgin, cheated death, and rose bodily into the heavens -- can now be eaten in the form of a cracker. A few Latin words spoken over your favorite Burgundy, and you

can drink his blood as well. Is there any doubt that a lone subscriber to these beliefs would be considered mad?

[Ibid.]

[e] It is time we acknowledged how disgraceful it is for the survivors of a catastrophe to believe themselves spared by a loving God, while this same God drowned infants in their cribs. Once you stop swaddling the reality of the world's suffering in religious fantasies, you will feel in your bones just how precious life is -- and, indeed, how unfortunate it is that millions of human beings suffer the most harrowing abridgements of their happiness for no good reason at all.

[Letter To A Christian Nation]

[f] What if a religion said: "Treat everyone well, don't lie, raise your children to excel in science and mathematics and if you don't do that, you're going to be tortured for eternity by a green-headed demon"? This would be a benign religion to spread when you compare it to the jihadist lunacy that goes on under the name of Islam or many of these end-time beliefs that animate Christianity at the moment. This would be a good religion, yet it wouldn't lend the slightest bit of credence to the claim that there's a demon who's going to enforce its precepts. People would recognize that immediately. It's based on this false notion that you can believe things simply because they're useful. You should only be able to believe things because you have reason to believe that they're true. Usefulness and truth are quite distinct. We can get our useful structures without deluding ourselves about the nature of the universe.

[Rochester City News, 18 October 2006]

Judith Hayes
(1945-   )

[g] If a plane crashes and 99 people die while 1 survives, it is called a miracle. Should the families of the 99 think so?

[In God We Trust:
But Which One?]

[h] If we are going to teach "creation science" as an alternative to evolution, then we should also teach the stork theory as an alternative to biological reproduction.

[Ibid.]

[i] The biblical account of Noah's Ark and the Flood is perhaps the most implausible story for fundamentalists to defend. Where, for example, while loading his ark, did Noah find penguins and polar bears in Palestine?

[Ibid.]

[j] [I]t wouldn't matter if every single President since Washington had been a Bible-toting, evangelical Christian. They weren't, of course, but even if they had been, it still would not change the secular foundation of our republic. Christians like to quote various Presidents or Supreme Court Justices who (quite incorrectly) have referred to our "Christian nation." But what do those quotes prove? I could quote Richard Nixon, but would that prove that ours was intended to be a nation of crooks?

["All Those Christian Presidents"]

Georg Wilhelm Friedrich Hegel
(1770-1831)

[k] God is, as it were, the sewer into which all contradictions flow.

[Lectures on the History of Philosophy]

[l] We may affirm absolutely that nothing great in the world has been accomplished without passion.

[Philosophy of History. Introduction]

[m] When liberty is mentioned, we must always be careful to observe whether it is not really the assertion of private interests which is thereby designation.

[Ibid. Part IV, Sect. 3, Chap. 2]

Heinrich Heine
(1797-1856)

[n] I called the Devil and he came,
His face with wonder I must scan;
He is not ugly, he is not lame,
He is a delightful, charming man;
A man in his prime of life, in fact,
Courteous, engaging, and full of tact...

[Pictures of Travels --
The Return Home (no. 37)]

Robert A. Heinlein
(1907-1988)

[o] Don't appeal to mercy from God the Father up in the sky, little man, because he's not at home and never was at home, and couldn't care less. What you do with yourself, whether you are happy or unhappy-- live or die-- is strictly your business and the universe doesn't care. In fact you may be the universe and the only cause of all your troubles. But, at best, the most you can hope for is comradeship with comrades no more divine (or just as divine) as you are. So quit sniveling and face up to it -- 'Thou art God!'

[21 October 1960]

[p] The Bible is such a gargantuan collection of conflicting values that anyone can prove anything from it.

[The Number of the Beast]

[q] The Ten Commandments are for lame brains. The first five are solely for the benefit of the priests and the powers that be; the second five are half truths, neither complete nor adequate.

[To Sail Beyond the Sunset]

[r] Theology is never any help; it is searching in a dark cellar at midnight for a black cat that isn't there.

[JOB: A Comedy of Justice]

Roy Helton
(1886-ca. 1960)

[s] The power in these feet and hands is adequate for me, and in this atom of myself explodes what needs to be free.

[Come Back To Earth. II. Stanza. 1946]

Ernest Hemingway
(1899-1961)

[t] All thinking men are atheists.

[A Farewell To Arms]

William Ernest Henley
(1849-1903)

[u] Out of the night that covers me,
Black as the Pit from pole to pole,
I thank whatever gods may be
For my unconquerable soul.

[Echoes. IV, In Memoriam
R. T. Hamilton Bruce ("Invictus")]

[v] Under the blungeonings of chance
My head is bloodied, but unbowed.

[Ibid.]

[w] It matters not how strait the gate,
How charged with punishments the scroll,
I am the master of my fate;
I am the captain of my soul.

[Ibid.]

Patrick Henry
(1736-1799)

[x] ...nothing will preserve it [liberty] but downright force. Whenever you give up that force, you are ruined...

[During Virginia's ratification convention, 1788]

Katharine Hepburn
(1907-2003)

[y] I'm an atheist, and that's it.

[Ladies' Home Journal, October 1991]

Hericlitus
(ca. 544-483 B.C.E.)

[z] Those unmindful when they hear, for all they make of their intelligence, may be regarded as the walking dead.

[unsourced]

[a] War (conflict) is both king of all and father of all, and it has revealed some as gods, others as men; some it has made slaves, others free.

[unsourced]

[b] One should know that war (conflict) is common to all, and that strife is justice; and all things both come to pass and perish through strife.

[unsourced]

[c] They do not understand how that which differs with itself is in agreement: harmony consists of opposing tension, like that of the bow and lyre.

[unsourced]

[d] Sea water is the purest and most polluted: for fish it is drinkable and life giving; for men, undrinkable and destructive.

[unsourced]

Alexander Herzen
(1812-1870)

[e] All religions have based morality on obedience, that is to say, on voluntary slavery. That is why they have always been more pernicious than any political organization. For the latter makes use of violence. The former -- of the corruption of the will.

[From Another Shore, 1855]

Theodor Herzl
(1860-1904)

[f] When I remember thee in days to come, O Jerusalem, it will not be with pleasure. The musty deposits of 2,000 years of inhumanity, intolerance, and uncleanliness lie in the foul-smelling alleys... The amiable dreamer of Nazareth has only contributed to increasing the hatred... What superstition and fanaticism on every side!

[after a visit to Jerusalem in 1898]

John Heywood
(1497-1580)

[g] When the iron is hot, strike.

[Proverbes. Part I, Chap II]

[h] Burnt child fire dreadth.

[Proverbes. Part II, Chap II]

Aaron Hill
(1685-1750)

[i] Tender-handed stroke a nettle,
And it stings you for your pains;
Grasp it like a man of mettle,
And it soft as silk remains.

Tis the same with common natures;
Use 'em kindly, they rebel;
But be rough as nutmeg-graters,
And the rogues obey you well.

[Verses Written on a Window in Scotland]

Christopher Hitchens
(1949-   )

[j] Who wishes that there was a permanent, unalterable celestial despotism that subjected us to continual surveillance and could convict us of thought-crime, and who regarded us as its private property even after we died? How happy we ought to be, at the reflection that there exists not a shred of respectable evidence to support such a horrible hypothesis.

[The Portable Atheist]

[k] A true believer... must also claim to have at least an inkling of what that Supreme Being desires. I have been called arrogant myself in my time... but to claim that I am privy to the secrets of the universe and its creator -- that's beyond my conceit.

[Letters to a Young Contrarian]

Adolf Hitler
(1889-1945)

[l] And I can fight only for something that I love, love only what I respect, and respect only what I at least know.

[Mein Kampf]

[m] We are placed in this world on condition of an eternal struggle for daily bread, as beings to whom nothing shall be given and who owe their position as lords of the earth only to the genius and courage with which they know how to struggle for and defend it.

[Ibid.]

[n] Those who are physically and mentally unhealthy and unfit must not perpetuate their sufferings in the bodies of their children... it is a crime and a disgrace to make this affliction the worse by passing it on to innocent creatures out of a merely egotistic yearning.

[Ibid.]

[o] A majority can never replace the man... Just as a hundred fools do not make one wise man, an heroic decision is not likely to come from a hundred cowards.

[Ibid. Chap. 3]

[p] Strength lies not in defense but in attack.

[Ibid.]

[q] All propaganda has to be popular and has to adapt its spiritual level to the perception of the least intelligent of those towards whom it intends to direct itself.

[Ibid. Chap. 6]

[r] The great masses of the people... will more easily fall victims to a great lie than to a small one.

[Ibid. Chap. 10]

[s] In the morning and even during the day men's will power revolts with highest energy against an attempt at being forced under another's will and another's opinions. In the evening, however, they succumb more easily to the dominating force of a stronger will.

[Ibid. Chap 6]

**Thomas Hobbes
(1588-1679)**

[t] Good and evil are names that signify our appetites and aversions, which in different tempers, customs, and doctrines of men are different: and diverse men differ not only in their judgment on the senses of what is pleasant and unpleasant to the taste, smell, hearing, touch, and sight; but also of what is conformable or disagreeable to reason in the actions of common life. Nay, the same man, in diverse times, differs from himself; and one time praiseth, that is, calleth good, what another time he dispraiseth, and calleth evil...

[Leviathan]

[u] The right of Nature... is the liberty each man hath to use his own power for the preservation of his own nature, that is to say of his own life, and consequently of doing anything, which in his own judgment and reason he shall conceive to be the aptest means thereto.

[Ibid.]

[v] Immortality is a belief grounded upon other men's sayings, that they knew it supernaturally; or that they knew those who knew them that knew others that knew it supernaturally.

[unsourced]

Ralph Hodgson
(1871-1962)

[w] I saw with open eyes
Singing birds sweet
Sold in the shops
For the people to eat,
Sold in the shops of
Stupidity Street.

[Stupidity Street. Stanza 1]

Eric Hoffer
(1902-1983)

[x] The less justified a man is in claiming excellence for his own self, the more ready he is to claim all excellence for his nation, his religion, his race or his holy cause.
[The True Believer]

[y] Crude absurdities, trivial nonsense, and

sublime truths are equally potent in readying people for self-sacrifice if they are accepted as the sole, eternal truth.

[Ibid.]

[z] They want freedom from "the fearful burden of free choice," freedom from the arduous responsibility of realizing their ineffectual selves and shouldering the blame for the blemished product. They do not want freedom of conscience, but faith – blind, authoritarian faith.

[Ibid.]

[a] The creed whose legitimacy is most easily challenged is likely to develop the strongest proselytizing impulse. It is doubtful whether a movement which does not profess some preposterous and patently irrational dogma can be possessed of that zealous drive which "must either win men or destroy the world." It is also plausible that those movements with the greatest inner contradiction between profession and practice -- that is to say with a strong feeling of guilt -- are likely to be the most fervent in imposing their faith on others.

[Ibid.]

Baron d'Holbach
(1723-1789)

[b] All children are atheists – they have no idea of God.

[Good Sense, 1772]

[c] If the ignorance of nature gave birth to gods, the knowledge of nature is calculated to destroy them.

[The System Of Nature, 1770]

[d] Theology is but the ignorance of natural causes reduced to a system.

[Good Sense, 1753]

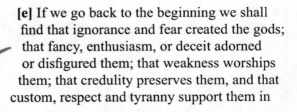

[e] If we go back to the beginning we shall find that ignorance and fear created the gods; that fancy, enthusiasm, or deceit adorned or disfigured them; that weakness worships them; that credulity preserves them, and that custom, respect and tyranny support them in

order to make the blindness of men serve its own interests.

[Ibid.]

R. J. Hollingdale
(1930-2001)

[f] ...the radical and universal consciousness of the death of God is still ahead of us; perhaps we shall have to colonize the stars before it is finally borne in upon us that God is not out there.

[Thomas Mann:
A Critical Study]

Oliver Wendell Holmes Sr.
(1809-1894)

[g] Rough work, iconoclasm, but the only way to get at truth.

[1860]

[h] Men are idolaters, and want something to look at and kiss, or throw themselves down before; they always did, they always will; and if you don't make it of wood, you must make it of words.

[The Poet At The Breakfast Table]

Elmer G. Homrighausen
(1900-1982)

[i] Few intelligent Christians can still hold to the idea that the Bible is an infallible book, that it contains no linguistic errors, no historical discrepancies, no antiquated scientific assumptions, not even bad ethical standards. Historical investigation and literary criticism have taken the magic out of the Bible and have made it a composite human book, written by many hands in different ages. The existence of thousands of variations of texts makes it impossible to hold the doctrine of a book verbally infallible. Some might claim for the original copies of the Bible an infallible character, but this view only begs the question and makes such Christian apologetics more ridiculous in the eyes of the sincere man.

[Christianity In America]

Herbert Clark Hoover
(1874-1964)

[j] No economic equality can survive the working of biological inequality.

[The Challenge to Liberty. Chap. 3]

Alfred Edward Housman
(1859-1936)

[k] And cowards' funerals, when they come,
Are not wept so well at home,
Therefore, though the best is bad,
Stand and do the best, my lad.

[A Shropshire Lad]

[l] The laws of God, the laws of man,
He may keep that will and can;
Not I: let God and man decree
Laws for themselves and not for me.

[Last Poems. XII]

Philip K. Howard
(1948-   )

[m] Modern law has not protected us from stupidity and caprice, but has made stupidity and caprice dominant features of our society.

[The Death of Common Sense]

Elbert Hubbard
(1856-1915)

[n] A miracle is an event described by those to whom it was told by people who did not see it.

[The Philistine, 1909]

[o] Dogma is a lie reiterated and authoritatively injected into the mind of one or more persons who believe that they believe what someone else believes.

[The Note Book, 1927]

[p] A mystic is a person who is puzzled before the obvious, but who understands the nonexistent.

[unsourced]

[q] Theology, by diverting the attention of men from this life to another, and by endeavoring to coerce all men into one religion, constantly preaching that this world is full of misery, but the next world would be beautiful -- or not, as the case may be -- has forced on men the thought of fear where otherwise there might have been the happy abandon of nature.

[unsourced]

William Henry Hudson
(1841-1922)

[r] When I meet with a falsehood, I care not who the great persons who proclaim it may be, I do not try to like it or believe it or mimic the fashionable prattle of the world about it.

[The Purple Land. Chap. 28]

Rupert Hughes
(1872-1956)

[s] According to the Bible, God was ignorant, a ruthless liar and cheat; he broke his pledges, changed his mind so often that he grew weary of repenting. He was a murderer of children, ordered his people to slay, rape, steal, and lie and commit every foul and filthy abomination in human power. In fact, the more I read the Bible the less I find in it that is either credible or admirable.

[Why I Quit Going To Church, 1924]

[t] The Christian religion has made the white man a blood-thirsty, cowardly, low-minded hypocrite, justifying all his foul acts with a Cross. Nothing but a club will keep the Christian fanatic out of government, out of the schools, out of control of press, theater, and police.

[letter to anonymous critic in Los Angeles]

[u] The Christians' god is to me non-existent. He is an idol fabricated in a brain enmeshed in the cobwebs of religious superstition. If he were the ideal spirit which they pretend to believe him, if he were all-wise, all-good, then every prayer uttered by a Christian is a blasphemy. If he were omniscient, omnipresent, omnipotent, he should need no guidance or control in the management of the little sphere on which we crawl from those who crawl. Does not the life of the pretender to a religious belief in almost every instance belie this pretended belief? If he were honest would he not shrink in horror at the fate which, according to his pretended belief, awaits the hypocrite and liar?

[letter to unknown critic]

Victor Hugo
(1802-1885)

[v] A saint addicted to excessive self-abnegation is a dangerous associate; he may infect you with poverty, and a stiffening of those joints which are needed for advancement -- in a word, with more renunciation than you care for -- and so you flee the contagion.

[Les Misérables]

[w] Popularity? It is glory's small change.

[Ruy Blas.
Act III, Sc. 5]

[x] There is in every village a torch: the schoolmaster -- and an extinguisher: the parson.

[unsourced]

Johan Huizinga
(1872-1945)

[y] We play, and know that we play, so we must be more than merely rational beings, for play is irrational... We find play present everywhere as a well-defined quality of action which is different from "ordinary" life.

[Homo Ludens]

David Hume
(1711-1776)

[z] A wise man proportions his belief to the

evidence.
[An Enquiry Concerning Human Understanding]

[a] The Christian religion not only was at first attended with miracles, but even at this day cannot be believed by any reasonable person without one.
[Ibid.]

**Aldous Huxley
(1894-1963)**

[b] In this second half of the twentieth century we do nothing systematic about our breeding; but in our random and unregulated way we are not only overpopulating our planet, we are also, it would seem, making sure that these greater numbers shall be of biologically poorer quality.
[Brave New World Revisited]

[c] The brotherhood of men does not imply their equality. Families have their fools and their men of genius, their black sheep and their saints, their worldly successes and their worldly failures.
[unsourced]

[d] If we must play the theological game, let us never forget that it is a game. Religion, it seems to me, can survive only as a consciously accepted system of make believe.
[Time Must Have A Stop]

[e] Defined in psychological terms, a fanatic is a man who consciously overcompensates a secret doubt.
[Proper Studies]

[f] Christianity accepted as given a metaphysical system derived from several already existing and mutually incompatible systems.
[Grey Eminence: A Study in Religion and Politics]

**Sir Julian Sorell Huxley
(1887-1975)**

[g] Operationally, God is beginning to resemble not a ruler but the last fading smile of a cosmic Cheshire Cat.

[Religion without Revelation]

Thomas Henry Huxley
(1825-1895)

[h] The rung of a ladder was never meant to rest upon, but only to hold a man's foot long enough to enable him to put the other somewhat higher.

[On Medical Education]

[i] It is the customary fate of new truths to begin as heresies and to end as superstitions.

[The Coming of Age of "The Origin of Species"]

[j] Skepticism is the highest duty and blind faith the one unpardonable sin.

[unsourced]

[k] The science, the art, the jurisprudence, the chief political and social theories, of the modern world have grown out of those of Greece and Rome -- not by favor of, but in the teeth of, the fundamental teachings of early Christianity, to which science, art, and any serious occupation with the things of this world, were alike despicable.

[Agnosticism and Christianity]

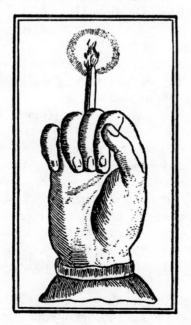

**Henrik Ibsen
(1828-1906)**

[l] Rob the average man of his life-illusion, and you rob him of his happiness in the same stroke.

[The Wild Duck. Act V]

[m] A lie, turned topsy-turvy, can be sprinkled and tinseled out, decked in plumage new and fine, till none knows its lean old carcass.

[Peer Gynt. Act I]

[n] It was then that I began to look into the seams of your doctrine. I wanted only to pick at a single knot; but when I had got that undone, the whole thing raveled out. And then I understood that it was all machine-sewn.

[Ghosts, Act II]

[o] The majority is never right. Never, I tell you! That's one of these lies in society that no free and intelligent man can help rebelling against. Who are the people that make up the biggest proportion of the population -- the intelligent ones or the fools? I think we can agree it's the fools, no matter where you go in this world, it's the fools that form the overwhelming majority.

[An Enemy of the People, Act IV]

[p] I'm plotting revolution against this lie that the majority has a monopoly of the truth.

What are these truths that always bring the majority rallying round? Truths so elderly they are practically senile. And when a truth is as old as that, gentlemen, you can hardly tell it from a lie.

[Ibid.]

Robert G. Ingersoll
(1833-1899)

[q] We are not endeavoring to chain the future but to free the present.... We are the advocates of inquiry, investigation, and thought.... It is grander to think and investigate for yourself than to repeat a creed... I look for the day when reason, throned upon the world's brains, shall be the King of Kings and the God of Gods.

["The Gods" 1872]

[r] We have heard talk enough. We have listened to all the drowsy, idealess, vapid sermons that we wish to hear. We have read your Bible and the works of your best minds. We have heard your prayers, your solemn groans and your reverential amens. All these amount to less than nothing. We want one fact. We beg at the doors of your churches for just one little fact. We pass our hats along your pews and under your pulpits and implore you for just one fact. We know all about your mouldy wonders and your stale miracles. We want a 'this year's fact.' We ask only one. Give us one fact for charity. Your miracles are too ancient. The witnesses have been dead for nearly two thousand years. Their reputation for 'truth and veracity' in the neighborhood where they resided is wholly unknown to us. Give us a new miracle, and substantiate it by witnesses who still have the cheerful habit of living this world. Do not send us to Jericho to hear the winding horns, nor put us in the fire with Shadrach, Meshech and Abednego. Do not compel us to navigate the sea with Captain Jonah, nor dine with Mr. Ezekiel. There is no sort of use in sending us fox-hunting with Samson. We have positively lost all interest in that little speech so eloquently delivered by Balaam's inspired donkey. It is worse than useless to show us fishes with money in their mouths, and call our attention to vast multitudes stuffing themselves with five crackers and two sardines. We demand a new miracle, and we demand it now. Let the church furnish at least one, or forever hold her peace.

[Ibid.]

[s] If the account given in Genesis is really true, ought we not, after all, to thank this serpent? He was the first schoolmaster, the first advocate of learning, the first enemy of ignorance, the first to whisper in human ears the sacred word liberty, the creator of ambition, the author of modesty, of inquiry, of doubt, of investigation, of progress and of civilization.

[Ibid.]

[t] The originality of repetition, and the mental vigor of acquiescence, are all that we have any right to expect from the Christian world. As long as every question is answered by the word "God," scientific inquiry is simply impossible. As fast as phenomena are satisfactorily explained the domain of the power, supposed to be superior to nature must decrease, while the horizon of the known must as constantly continue to enlarge.

[Ibid.]

[u] In every age some thinker, some doubter, some investigator, some hater of hypocrisy, some despiser of sham, some brave lover of the right, has gladly, proudly and heroically braved the ignorant fury of superstition for the sake of man and truth.

[Ibid.]

[v] This crime called blasphemy was invented by priests for the purpose of defending doctrines not able to take care of themselves.

[An Interview On Chief Justice Comegys]

[w] Every fact is an enemy of the church. Every fact is a heretic. Every demonstration is an infidel. Everything that ever really happened testifies against the supernatural.

[Orthodoxy, 1884]

[x] The religion of Jesus Christ, as preached by his church, causes war, bloodshed, hatred, and all uncharitableness; and why? Because, they say, a certain belief is necessary to salvation. They do not say, if you behave yourself you will get there; they do not say, if you pay your debts and love your wife and love your children, and are good to your friends, and your neighbors, and your country, you will get there; that will do you no good; you have got to believe a certain thing. No matter how bad you

are, you can instantly be forgiven; and no matter how good you are, if you fail to believe that which you cannot understand, the moment you get to the day of judgment nothing is left but to damn you, and all the angels will shout "hallelujah."

[Ibid.]

[y] The real oppressor, enslaver, and corrupter of the people is the Bible. That book is the chain that binds, the dungeon that holds the clergy. That book spreads the pall of superstition over the colleges and schools. That book puts out the eyes of science, and makes honest investigation a crime. That book fills the world with bigotry, hypocrisy and fear.

[Some Mistakes Of Moses]

[z] I have little confidence in any enterprise or business or investment that promises dividends only after the death of the stockholders.

[unsourced]

[a] I combat those only who, knowing nothing of the future, prophesy an eternity of pain -- those who sow the seeds of fear in the hearts of men -- those only who poison all the springs of life, and seat a skeleton at every feast.

[unsourced]

[b] If a man would follow, today, the teachings of the Old Testament, he would be a criminal. If he would follow strictly the teachings of the New [Testament], he would be insane.

[unsourced]

[c] Our civilization is not Christian. It does not come from the skies. It is not a result of "inspiration." It is the child of invention, of discovery, of applied knowledge -- that is to say, of science.

["Reply To The Indianapolis Clergy," The Iconoclast, 1882]

[d] In nature there are neither rewards nor punishments; there are consequences.

["The Christian Religion," 1881]

[e] ...to argue with a man who has renounced his reason is like giving medicine to the dead.

[Ingersoll's Works. Vol. 1, p.127]

[f] The inspiration of the Bible depends on the ignorance of the person who reads it.

[The Ingersoll-Black Debate, 25 April 1881]

[g] The man who does not do his own thinking is a slave, and is a traitor to himself and to his fellow-men.

[The Liberty Of Man, Woman And Child]

[h] Tell me there is a God in the serene heavens that will damn his children for the expression of an honest belief! More men have died in their sins, judged by your orthodox creeds, than there are leaves on all the forests in the wide world ten thousand times over. Tell me these men are in hell; that these men are in torment; that these children are in eternal pain, and that they are to be punished forever and forever! I denounce this doctrine as the most infamous of lies.

[Ibid.]

Mary Jean Irion
(?-?)

[i] Christianity... has been over for a hundred years now... When something even so small as a lightbulb goes out, the eyes for a moment still see it; and a sound after it is made will have, in the right places, an echo. So it is not at all strange that when something so huge as a world religion goes out, there remains for a century or more in certain places some notion that it is still there.

[From the Ashes of Christianity, 1968]

Washington Irving
(1783-1859)

[j] Your true dull minds are generally preferred for public employ, and especially promoted to city honors; your keen intellects, like razors, being considered too sharp for common service.

[Knickerbocker's History of New York.
Book III, Chap. 2]

William James
(1842-1910)

[k] The arguments for God's existence have stood for hundreds of years with the waves of unbelieving criticism breaking against them, never totally discrediting them in the ears of the faithful, but on the whole slowly and surely washing out the mortar from between their joints.

[The Varieties of Religious Experience, 1902]

Thomas Jefferson
(1743-1826)

[l] In every country and in every age, the priest has been hostile to liberty. He is always in alliance with the despot, abetting his abuses in return for protection to his own.

[letter to Horatio Spafford, 17 March 1814]

[m] It does me no injury for my neighbor to say there are twenty gods or no god. It neither picks my pocket nor breaks my leg.

[Notes On The State Of Virginia, 1782]

[n] I have examined all the known superstitions of the world, and I do not find in our particular superstition of Christianity one redeeming feature. They are all alike founded on fables and mythology. Millions of inno-

cent men, women and children, since the introduction of Christianity, have been burnt, tortured, fined and imprisoned. What has been the effect of this coercion? To make one half the world fools and the other half hypocrites; to support roguery and error all over the earth.

[letter to William Short]

[o] [I do not believe in] the immaculate conception of Jesus, his deification, the creation of the world by him, his miraculous powers, his resurrection and visible ascension, his corporeal presence in the Eucharist, the Trinity; original sin, atonement, regeneration, election, orders of the Hierarchy, etc.

[letter to William Short, 31 October 1819]

[p] Christianity... (has become) the most perverted system that ever shone on man... perverted into an engine for enslaving mankind...

[to Samuel Kercheval, 1810]

[q] The day will come when the mystical generation of Jesus, by the Supreme Being as his father, in the womb of a virgin, will be classed with the fable of the generation of Minerva in the brain of Jupiter.

[letter to John Adams]

[r] To talk of immaterial existences is to talk of nothings. To say that the human soul, angels, god, are immaterial, is to say they are nothings, or that there is no god, no angels, no soul.

[letter to John Adams, 15 August 1820]

[s] I do not believe in the creed professed by the Jewish church, by the Roman church, by the Greek church, by the Turkish church, by the Protestant church, nor by any church that I know of. My own mind is my own church.

[unsourced]

[t] I am for freedom of religion and against all maneuvers to bring about a legal ascendancy of one sect over another.

[to Elbridge Gerry, 1799]

[u] Question with boldness even the existence of God; because if there be one, He must approve the homage of Reason rather than that of blindfolded Fear.

[letter to Peter Carr, 10 Aug. 1787]

[v] They [priests] have tried upon me all their various batteries of pious whining, hypocritical canting, lying and slandering. I have contemplated their order from the Magi of the East to the Saints of the West and I have found no difference of character, but of more or less caution, in proportion to their information or ignorance on whom their interested duperies were to be played off. Their sway in New England is indeed formidable. No mind beyond mediocrity dares there to develop itself.

[letter to Horatio Spafford, 1816]

[w] Because religious belief or non-belief is such an important part of every person's life, freedom of religion affects every individual. State churches that use government power to support themselves and force their views on persons of other faiths undermine all our civil rights. Moreover, state support of the church tends to make the clergy unresponsive to the people and leads to corruption within religion. Erecting the "wall of separation between church and state," therefore, is absolutely essential in a free society.

[letter to Virginia Baptists, 1808]

Penn Jillette
(1955-   )

[x] Believing there's no God means I can't really be forgiven except by kindness and faulty memories. That's good; it makes me want to be more thoughtful. I have to try to treat people right the first time around.

["There Is No God"]

Wei Jingsheng
(1950-   )

[y] We want to be masters of our own destiny. We need no gods or emperors. We do not believe in the existence of any saviour. We want to be masters of the world and not instruments used by autocrats to carry out their wild ambitions...

["The Fifth Modernisation: Democracy and Other Issues"]

Cyril Edwin Mitchinson Joad
(1891-1953)

[z] There are those who feel an imperative need

to believe, for whom the values of a belief are proportionate not to its truth, but to its definiteness. Incapable of either admitting the existence of contrary judgments or of suspending their own, they supply the place of knowledge by turning other men's conjectures into dogmas.

[The Recovery Of Belief]

Hewlett Johnson
(1874-1966)

[a] Not so easily does a people liberate itself from its social past. Many ideas, customs, intolerances, and tolerances, too, cling on unperceived by those who think that they live in days where all things are new.

[The Soviet Power: The Socialist Sixth of the World. Book II:2]

Samuel Johnson
(1709-1784)

[b] As the Spanish proverb says, "He, who would bring home the wealth of the Indies, must carry the wealth of the Indies with him," so it is in traveling, a man must carry knowledge with him if he would bring home knowledge.

[Boswell's Life of Dr. Johnson. Volume II]

John Paul Jones
(1747-1792)

[c] I have not yet begun to fight.

[Aboard the Bonhomme Richard. 23 September 1779]

James Joyce
(1882-1941)

[d] Broken heart. A pump after all, pumping thousands of gallons of blood every day. One fine day it gets bunged up and there you are.... Old rusty pumps: damn the thing else. The resurrection and the life. Once you are dead you are dead.

[Ulysses]

[e] He comes into the world God knows how, walks on the water, gets out of his grave and

goes up off the Hill of Howth. What drivel is this?

[Stephen Hero]

Carl Jung
(1875-1961)

[f] Archetypes are like riverbeds which dry up when the water deserts them, but which it can find again at any time.

["Wotan"]

Wendy Kaminer
(1950-   )

[g] If I were to mock religious belief as childish, if I were to suggest that worshipping a supernatural deity, convinced that it cares about your welfare, is like worrying about monsters in the closet who find you tasty enough to eat, if I were to describe God as our creation, likening him to a mechanical gorilla, I'd violate the norms of civility and religious correctness. I'd be excoriated as an example of the cynical, liberal elite responsible for America's moral decline. I'd be pitied for my spiritual blindness; some people would try to enlighten and convert me. I'd receive hate mail. Atheists generate about as much sympathy as pedophiles. But, while pedophilia may at least be characterized as a disease, atheism is a choice, a willful rejection of beliefs to which vast majorities of people cling.

["The Last Taboo"]

Walter Kaufmann
(1921-1980)

[h] Theology was founded by Plato and Aristotle, who eulogized their highest principles by calling them divine. Theology is an impertinence perpetuated by a couple of philosophers.

[Critique of Religion
and Philosophy]

Omar Khayyám
(1048-1131)

[i] Men talk of heaven, -- there is no heaven but here;
Men talk of hell, -- there is no hell but here;
Men of hereafters talk, and future lives, --
O love, there is no other life -- but here.

[Rubáiyát]

[j] Look not above, there is no answer there;
Pray not, for no one listens to your prayer;
NEAR is as near to God as any FAR,
And HERE is just the same deceit as THERE.

[Ibid.]

Søren Kierkegaard
(1813-1855)

[k] Christianity demands the crucifixion of the intellect.
[quoted in Morals Without Religion by Margaret Knight]

[l] Christendom has done away with Christianity, without being quite aware
of it...

[as cited in Time,
16 December 1946]

Florence King
(1936-   )

[m] Our [society's] feminized niceness has mired us in a soft, sickly, helpless
tolerance of everything. America is the girl who can't say no, the town pump
who lets anybody have a go at her. We are a single-parent country with no father to cut through the molasses and point out, for
example, the inconsistency of embracing warm
and compassionate "values" while condemn-
ing cold and detached "value judgments."
[With Charity
Toward None]

[n] Most misanthropes are easy to understand

because we blurt out the simple truths that most people think but never say. The plainspoken have nothing to lose but their friends, so we weigh the risks and behave accordingly.

[Ibid.]

[o] Insecurity breeds treachery: if you are kind to people who hate themselves, they will hate you as well. It does no good to try to help them because they never really change no matter how long they stay in therapy... Insecure people are dangerous and it is best to stay away from them... only a misanthrope can avoid being exsanguinated by their emotional demands.

[Ibid.]

[p] I expect old age to suit me even better because there is so much leeway. The younger a misanthrope is, the less he -- and especially she -- can get away with. I long ago learned that no young woman can be an eccentric; people simply will not accept it. Oblique behavior and outlandish statements from a woman of twenty or thirty are greeted with speechless fury, but when she does and says the same things fifty years later, everyone smiles indulgently and says, "Oh, well, she's old."

[Ibid.]

Rudyard Kipling
(1865-1936)

[q] The Three in One, the One in Three? Not so! To my own Gods I go. It may be they shall give me greater ease than your cold Christ and tangled Trinities.

["Lispeth." 1888]

[r] Now these are the Laws of the Jungle, and many and mighty are they; But the head and the hoof of the Law and the haunch and the hump is -- Obey!

[The Law of the Jungle.
Refrain]

[s] Many religious people are deeply suspicious. They seem -- for purely religious purposes, of course -- to know more about iniquity than the Unregenerate.

[Plain Tales.
Watchers of the Night]

The Wonders of the Invisible World.

OBSERVATIONS

As well *Historical* as *Theological*, upon the NATURE, the
NUMBER, and the OPERATIONS of the

DEVILS.

Accompany'd with,

I. Some Accounts of the Grievous Molestations, by DÆ-
MONS and WITCHCRAFTS, which have lately
annoy'd the Countrey; and the Trials of some eminent
Malefactors Executed upon occasion thereof: with several
Remarkable *Curiosities* therein occurring.

II. Some Counsils, Directing a due Improvement of the terrible things, lately done, by the Unusual & Amazing
Range of EVIL SPIRITS, in Our Neighbourhood: &
the methods to prevent the *Wrongs* which those *Evil
Angels* may intend against all sorts of people among us.
especially in Accusations of the Innocent.

III. Some Conjectures upon the great EVENTS, likely
to befall, the WORLD in General, and NEW EN-
GLAND in Particular; as also upon the Advances of
the TIME, when we shall see BETTER DAYES.

IV. A short Narrative of a late Outrage committed by a
knot of WITCHES in *Swedeland*, very much Resem-
bling, and so far Explaining, *That* under which our parts
of *America* have laboured!

V. THE DEVIL DISCOVERED: In a Brief Discourse upon
those TEMPTATIONS, which are the more Ordinary *Devices*
of the Wicked One.

By Cotton Mather.

Boston Printed by *Benj. Harris* for *Sam. Phillips*. 1693.

Margaret Knight
(1903-1983)

[t] Jesus exhorted his followers to "become as little children," and the Church throughout history has extolled credulity, and feared and distrusted the free intelligence. During the Dark Ages the Church was in control of education, and for centuries scarcely anyone who was not a potential priest learned to read or write. One of the most persistent fallacies about the Christian Church is that it kept learning alive during the Dark and Middle Ages. What the Church did was to keep learning alive in the monasteries, while preventing the spread of knowledge outside them.

[Christianity, The Debit Account.
1975]

Arthur Koestler
(1905-1983)

[u] I have repeatedly stressed that the selfish impulses of man constitute a much less historic danger than his integrative tendencies. To put it in the simplest way: the individual who indulges in an excess of aggressive self-assertiveness incurs the penalties of society -- he outlaws himself, he contracts out of the hierarchy. The true believer, on the other hand, becomes more closely knit into it; he enters the womb of his church, or party, or whatever the social holon to which he surrenders his identity.

[The Ghost in the Machine]

Jiddu Krishnamurti
(1895-1986)

[v] ...your belief in God is merely an escape from your monotonous, stupid and cruel life.

[Krishnamurti's Talks
1949-1950]

Stanley Kubrick
(1928-1999)

[w] The whole idea of God is absurd.
[interview from
American Cinematographer, 1963]

Paul Kurtz
(1925-   )

[x] ...in the final analysis it is the theist who can find no ultimate meaning in this life and who denigrates it... The theist can only find meaning by leaving this life for a transcendental world beyond the grave.

[The Transcendental Temptation]

[y] The skeptic has no illusions about life, nor a vain belief in the promise of immortality. Since this life here and now is all we can know, our most reasonable option is to live it fully.

[Ibid.]

Kenneth V. Lanning
(?-?)

[z] The fact is that far more crime and child abuse has been committed by zealots in the name of God, Jesus and Mohammed than has ever been committed in the name of Satan. Many people, including myself, don't like that statement, but the truth of it is undeniable.

[FBI Report - Satanic Ritual Abuse, 1992]

[a] Nothing is more simple than "the devil made them do it." If we do not understand something, we make it the work of some supernatural force. During the Middle Ages, serial killers were thought to be vampires and werewolves, and child sexual abuse was the work of demons taking the form of parents and clergy.

[Ibid.]

Corliss Lamont
(1902-1995)

[b] God, once imagined to be an omnipresent force throughout the whole world of nature and man, has been increasingly tending to seem omniabsent. Everywhere, intelligent and educated people rely more and more on purely secular and scientific techniques for the solution of their problems. As science

advances, belief in divine miracles and the efficacy of prayer becomes fainter and fainter.

[The Philosophy of Humanism]

Robert A. Lang
(1966-   )

[c] This [God] character creates mankind with all of its intricacies, emotions, needs and desires and then demands that his creation deny its very nature. That is like creating a cat and telling it not to meow or you will kill it.

[Something Cool News #52, March 2004]

[d] We [Satanists] cherish the idea that Satan represents the opposition to all that Christianity, other spiritual religions and certain movements stand for. Those who cannot see that or are simply incapable of setting aside their hang-ups with a word like Satan are not the kind of people we [the Church of Satan] are interested in.

[Ibid.]

[e] Nature has its way of dealing with shabby architecture, badly mixed cement and inattentive gazelles.

["The Confederacy of Newspeak..."]

Anton Szandor LaVey
(1930-1997)

[f] I don't feel that raising the Devil in an anthropomorphic sense is quite as feasible as theologians or metaphysicians would like to think. I have felt his presence but only as an exteriorized extension of my own potential, as an alter ego or evolved concept that I have been able to exteriorize. With a full awareness, I can communicate with this semblance, this creature, this demon, this personification that I see in the eyes of the symbol of Satan -- the Goat of Mendes -- as I commune with him before the altar. None of these is anything more than a mirror image of that potential I perceive in myself.

[interview from Popular Witchcraft
by Jack Fritscher]

[g] Christ has failed in all his engagements as

both savior and deity. If his doctrines were that easily misinterpreted, if his logic was that specious, let's throw it out. It has no place. It is worthless to a civilized society if it is subject to gross misinterpretation.

[Ibid.]

[h] Most writings about Satanism are written by people whose emotional survival is every bit as dependent upon cherished lies as their readers... the blind leading the blind.

[interview printed in Black Magic, Satanism and Voodoo by Dr. Leo L. Martello]

[i] The popular mind has never displayed an overabundance of objectivity. The popular mind accepts most data with little or no question, unless it happens to hurt. Then it is rejected.

[Ibid.]

[j] I believe in the glorification of the ego. That is a good separation process. A pumped-up, overinflated ego will display a fool's flaws quickly and put him out of the running, while the worthy will rise to meet the added responsibilities that will accompany their exaltation.

[Ibid.]

[k] Drugs are great for the slaves, but no good for the Masters. The glories attained through a drug experience are no more valid than the meaningless baubles with which the status-seeking drone surrounds himself... Those who eulogize on unfoldment gained through drugs have obviously been insensitive to such awareness-provoking stimuli as complete sexual fulfillment, beautiful music, inspirational literature, etc. The excuse that certain drugs are a necessary adjunct to the practice of magic is quite lame.

[Ibid.]

[l] I consider drug abuse a polite alternative to suicide. Perhaps one day euthanasia will be made attractive enough and the drug problem will be solved.

[Ibid.]

[m] The most equal of all human beings, I would say, would be on the lowest level... But when you get higher up on the evolutionary scale -- or social order, whichever you

prefer -- you're going to find more differentiation in human beings as you ascend. And then, of course, the higher you go up, the more unequal you find those from the ones at the bottom. What is usually meant by "equality" is really "common denominators."

[interview from Answer ME! Issue 2]

[n] I wouldn't squash a spider, but I could kill a human being. A spider is being the best spider he can be. He's fulfilling his purpose as a spider. He meshes perfectly with nature's overall scheme. Nothing in nature is wasted, and I can't say the same thing about people.

[Ibid.]

[o] These endless occult degrees are just a substitute for achievement in the real world. It's the same thing when you get one performer who can't perform and is stupid, and they'll praise another who also can't perform. That's the conspiracy of ineptitude.

[interview from The Black Flame. Vol. 5, #s 3 and 4]

[p] It's a magical principle that when everybody is tapping into something at the same time it dilutes the magical power it might have. It decreases its value. It's like, if everybody looks the same, how do you know when someone is beautiful?

[interview from Ben Is Dead. Issue 25]

[q] Any vested interest which contrivedly interferes with your best interests is THEY.

["They" from The Black Flame. Vol. 6, #s 1 & 2]

[r] Those who are humorless should not be taken seriously. They take themselves so seriously, they leave no room for others to do likewise.

[Satan Speaks]

[s] Wit, like style, is not an acquired commodity.
One either has it or does not.

[Ibid.]

[t] When I say, "I am a very happy man in a compulsively unhappy world," it is because I clearly see that others wish to impose their masochistic needs upon me. It becomes a rejec-

tion of attempted conversion to a system I want no part of.

[Ibid.]

[u] Only a fool mistakes laughter for humor and fashion for style.

[Ibid.]

[v] One of the reasons I hate people so much is because they are basically an insecure, treacherous, dishonest lot. Gossip and soap opera are nothing more than a reflection of their daily lives: filled with sour grapes, nit-picking, belittling, and every manner of envy. No wonder those despicable traits have led to incurable greed. Whether on a grubby little get-something-for-nothing, win-the-lottery level, or on a corporate and political level, there is complete disregard for the lives of the most valuable fellow humans.

[Ibid.]

[w] The world is NOT a stage upon which we are all actors playing a part. In this world, there are the performers and there is the audience. They are never interchangeable. The members of the audience are the followers. The performers are the leaders. If a person is one, there is no chance that he can become the other.

[Ibid.]

[x] We are engulfed in war. Not simply a war fought with guns and bombs "somewhere out there." The skirmishes take place in the region of one's own mind. The less one is aware of the invisible war, the more receptive one is to its ongoing process of demoralization, for the insensate human is vulnerable, malleable, weak and ripe for control.

["The Invisible War" from Apocalypse Culture]

[y] With all the good wine in the world, it always fails to amaze me how many people raise sour grapes.

["Backlash" from The Cloven Hoof. Volume VIII, #3. May/June XI A.S.]

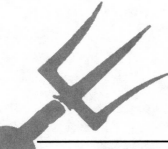

[z] ...Without the Church of Satan, sensation-seekers, human barnacles, Chicken Littles, and unimaginative lumpenvolk might have to return to what Donald Corley called "The House of Lost Identity." And that, my dear Satanists, is why Satanism sells to the masses,

especially in its sillytickle "truth." Don't knock it too much. They need us far more than we need them. What would they do without us?

["The 'Truth' Hurts" from The Cloven Hoof.
Volume VIII, #5. Sept./Oct. XI A.S.]

[a] The difference between a talker and a storyteller is that the talker utters data of varying degrees of pertinence and relevance. A shaman or storyteller (magician, perhaps) imparts relevance to whatever he says so that his listener will care, even if he has no inherent or acquired interest in the topic.

["Trivia Unchained" from The Cloven Hoof.
Volume IX, #6. Nov./Dec. XII A.S.]

[b] One of the real reasons why little is presently happening of originality is arrogance born of imagined self-importance. When everyone is a VIP and everything is something, complacency and stagnation ensue. The only respite from the Good Life is in reverie or speculation.

["What's New? Not Much" from
The Cloven Hoof. Vol. X, #4. July/Aug XIII A.S.]

[c] If you profess to be a Satanist and aren't somewhat removed from the mainstream of popular culture in your personal tastes and beliefs, then perhaps you should reexamine the philosophical meaning of Satanism and whether it indeed applies to yourself.

["More on Phase Six..." from
The Cloven Hoof. Vol. XI, #3. May/June of XIV A.S.]

[d] I don't find popular pursuits distasteful per se, only the hysteria which accompanies them. Yet I also realize that without that very popularity, less unification of the herd would transpire, leading to chaos and loss of control. That is why I recognize a need for popular pursuits and would do nothing to discourage them. Just count me out.

["Today's Madness Is Tomorrow's Norm"
from The Cloven Hoof. Vol. XII, #2/3.
March/April/May/June of XV A.S.]

[e] I know full well the brutality and cruelty of which I am capable, so I stay away from things which anger me. Not that I am doing society any favors. On the contrary; If I were to become the fiend or berserker of which I

know -- if I should perform some hideous tasks, thereby calling attention to myself -- then I would give cheap entertainment to others who are far more intrinsically vicious than myself. And I would become their slave, their jester, their release from boredom. I am too selfish for that.

["We're All Going Calling On The Kaiser..." from The Cloven Hoof. Vol. XII, #2/3. March/April/May/June of XV A.S.]

[f] Sex, religion, and cosmetics are commodities that will always sell. Of the three, religion exhibits the most appalling lack of variety. One would think that the God racket could produce the diversity of merchandise that other industries concoct. No such luck. If variety is the spice of life, the bland cuisine served up by the chefs of theology is as tasteless as it is deathly. Still, like mush, it is gobbled up by the hungry.

["Religion -- or -- The Goddess is Made Of Polyurethane Foam" from The Cloven Hoof. Vol. XII, #2/3. March/April/May/June of XV A.S.]

[g] A magician has only two choices: accept the subjective world of others and manipulate within its framework, or create a subjective world of his own and go at it with such daring and self-confidence that through contagion it will then become the idealized world of others.

[from The Cloven Hoof. Vol. XIII, #2. March/April XVI A.S.]

[h] The validity of any praise should always be considered in relation to its source. Praise from a fool is less than worthless. It is misleading. The only value of a fool is as a recipient for the assertion of one's will.

[from The Cloven Hoof. Vol. XIII, #3. May/June XVI A.S.]

[i] I don't really mind it when someone I consider inferior tries to bring me down to his level. What annoys me is when he heavy-footedly attempts to elevate himself to mine.

[from The Cloven Hoof. Vol. XIII, #4. Sept/Oct XVI A.S.]

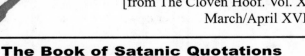

[j] Satanism is more than a philosophy; it is a lone stand, a symbolic act of defiance against thought suppression.

[from The Cloven Hoof. Vol. XIV, #3. March/April XVII A.S.]

[k] The best means to lull someone into acceptance is to allow him to feel he is All Right. The rest will take care of itself. If a person can't be famous, it doesn't matter as long as he thinks he's All Right. Being right is an acceptable substitute for personal achievement. That's why the most pious are generally the least accomplished.

> [from The Cloven Hoof. Vol. XIV, #5. Sept/Oct XVII A.S.]

[l] I consider it my unhallowed duty to present an alternative to any cause, trend, or pursuit which results in mass mindlessness. Don't get me wrong! I'm all for mass mindlessness -- for the masses. But not for myself or the Chosen Few. If someone didn't present an alternative, nothing would ever change. Yet, even though I consider such advocacy a duty, I come by it quite naturally. The thought of being like everyone else is repellent.

> [from The Cloven Hoof. Vol. XV, #5. Sept/Oct XVIII A.S.]

[m] Trendiness is seldom stimulating. Comfortable, yes, but not stimulating. Comfort can only run second place to stimulation. Too much comfort leads to ennui. That's why most people can only stand a limited amount of happiness. When their happiness becomes unendurable, they take to fighting among themselves in order to experience a break from monotony.

> [from The Cloven Hoof. Vol. XVI, #6. Nov/Dec XIX A.S.]

[n] Some terrific test passers are mental pygmies with just enough room in their brains for whatever information is required to get a high score. A year later, they've forgotten whatever they learned to pass the test. But they can pass their new one just fine.

> ["Don't Recycle Your Brain"
> from The Cloven Hoof. Vol. XIX, #1. Issue 115]

[o] What happens when the strong take lessons from the weak? The superior are pragmatically adaptive. They will emulate those traits, augment them, and destroy the weak with the very tools the weak have given them. The inferior should have thought of that in the first place, but then -- if they could have, they wouldn't be inferior.

> ["A Lesson To Be Learned"
> from The Cloven Hoof.
> Vol. XXI, #2. Issue 124]

[p] Mystery religions will always exist in one

form or another. Their followers don't really want to know the answers, for their world view is based not on what they know and can do, but what they don't know, and are not expected to do. So long as they can say they are "seeking," they will be off the hook. "Seeking" implies "trying" and, like "good sportsmanship," they need never succeed so long as they are trying. A Satanist "tries" once, and if it doesn't work, moves on to something that will. The same mentality that makes a professional student motivates the "seeker."

[*"The Last Mystery" from The Cloven Hoof. Issue 129]

[q] The hunter must hunt. The moment he stops he becomes the hunted.

[The Devil's Notebook]

[r] After an inferior man has been taught a doctrine of superiority he will remain as inferior as he was before his lesson. He will merely assume himself to be superior, and attempt to employ his recently-learned tactics against his own kind, whom he will then consider his inferiors. With each inferior man enjoying what he considers his unique role, the entire bunch will be reduced to a pack of strutting, foppish, self-centered monkeys gamboling about on an island of ignorance. There they will play their games under the supervision of their keeper, who was and will always be a superior man.

[Ibid.]

[s] Self-improvement books: those who need them won't read them or heed them.

[Ibid.]

[t] The true test of anyone's worth as a living creature is how much he can utilize what he has.

[Ibid.]

[u] Right, like water, seeks its own level. Man's consent is not necessary to the operations of Satanic Forces. It is not required. It is not even asked.

[Ibid.]

[v] Sometimes the reality of Satanism is a lot more terrifying to people than their safe fantasies of what it's supposed to be. For the first time, they've been confronted with a Devil that talks back.

[The Satanic Bible]

[w] Now it is the higher man's role to produce the children of the future. Quality is now more important than quantity. One cherished child who can create will be more important than two who can produce -- or fifty who can believe!

[The Satanic Rituals]

[x] Here are some reasons why it is called "Satanism:" It is most stimulating under that name, and self-discipline and motivation are easier under stimulating conditions. It means "the opposition" and epitomizes all symbols of non-conformity. It represents the strongest ability to turn a liability into an advantage -- to turn alienation into exclusivity. In other words, the reason it's called "Satanism" is because it's fun, it's accurate and it's productive.

[quoted from The Church of Satan by Blanche Barton]

David Herbert Lawrence
(1885-1930)

[y] Be a good animal, true to your animal instincts.

[The White Peacock]

[z] I never saw a wild thing sorry for itself.

[Self-Pity]

[a] Necessary, for ever necessary, to burn out false shames and smelt the heaviest ore of the body into purity.

[Lady Chatterley's Lover]

Gustave Le Bon
(1841-1931)

[b] To attribute to others the identical sentiments that guide oneself is never to understand others.

[Gustave Le Bon:
The Man and His Works]

[c] One of the greatest illusions of democracy is to imagine that instruction equalizes men. It often serves only to emphasize their differentiation.

[Ibid.]

[d] A brutal darling minority will always lead a fearful, irresolute majority.

[Ibid.]

[e] Crowds generally prefer equality in servitude to liberty.

[Ibid.]

[f] People who have not acquired an internal discipline are condemned to submit to an external discipline.

[Ibid.]

[g] Nature does not recognize equality. The only progress has been through increasing inequalities.

[Ibid.]

[h] To live is to struggle. Struggle is universal. Non-combative beings would have made no progress.

[Ibid.]

[i] From the dawn of civilization onwards, crowds have always undergone the influence of illusions... The masses have never thirsted after truth. They turn aside from evidence that is not to their taste, preferring to deify error, if error seduce them. Whoever can supply them with illusions is easily their master; whoever attempts to destroy illusions is always their victim.

[The Crowd]

Fran Lebowitz
(1950-   )

[j] All God's children are not beautiful. Most of God's children are, in fact, barely presentable.

[Metropolitan Life]

William Edward Hartpole Lecky
(1838-1903)

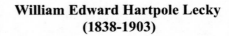

[k] All history shows that, in exact proportion as nations advance in civilization, the accounts of miracles taking place among them become rarer and rarer, until at last they entirely cease.

[History of the Rise and Influence of the Spirit of Rationalism in Europe]

Gypsy Rose Lee
(1914-1970)

[l] Praying is like a rocking chair -- it'll give you something to do, but it won't get you anywhere.

[unsourced]

John Lennon
(1940-1980)

[m] Christianity will go. It will vanish and shrink. I needn't argue about that. I'm right and I will be proved right.

[London Evening Standard. 4 March 1966]

James Henry Leuba
(1867-1946)

[n] It is, furthermore, essential to intellectual and moral advances that the beliefs that come into existence should have free play. Antagonistic beliefs must have the chance of proving their worth in open contest. It is this way scientific theories are tested, and in this way also, religious and ethical conceptions should be tried. But a fair struggle cannot take place when people are dissuaded from seeking knowledge, or when knowledge is hidden.

[quoted in David Brooks, The Necessity of Atheism]

Clive Staples Lewis
(1898-1963)

[o] Of all tyrannies, a tyranny exercised for the good of its victims may be the most oppressive. It may be better to live under robber barons than under omnipotent moral busybodies. The robber baron's cruelty may sometimes sleep, his cupidity may at some point be satiated; but those who torment us for our own good will torment us without end, for they do so with the approval of their own conscience.

["God in the Dock"]

Joseph Lewis
(1889-1968)

[p] Man's atonement consists in making himself as miserable as possible by praying, fasting, masochism, flagellations and other forms of torture. This sadistic delusion causes him to insist that others -- under pain of punishment -- be as miserable as himself, for fear that if others fail to do as he does, it will provoke the wrath of his tyrant God to a more severe chastisement. The inevitable result is that Man devotes his life, not to the essentials of living and the making of a happy home, but to the building of temples and churches where he can "lift his voice to God" in a frenzy of fanaticism, and eventually he becomes a victim of hysteria. His time and energy are wasted to cleanse his "soul," which he does not possess, and to save himself from a future punishment in hell which exists only in his imagination.

[An Atheist Manifesto, 1954]

[q] Is it not better to place a question mark upon a problem while seeking an answer than to put the label "God" there and consider the matter closed?

[The Philosophy Of Atheism]

[r] Of the ten crimes which Biblical Hebrew law punished by stoning, nine have ceased to be offenses in modern society.

[The Ten Commandments]

[s] On too many occasions, especially in matters concerning purported conversations and messages from gods, mystery has been employed by charlatans to hoodwink the people.

[Ibid.]

G. Gordon Liddy
(1930-   )

[t] ...One was a man who, having been shot with a 9mm slug that embedded so close to his spine, it was never removed, blew the man who put it there out of a phone booth with all six rounds from a .357 magnum. I relate to people like that.

[Will]

[u] My last fear, the fear of God, died with my faith. I was now alone and would have to live life armed only with my own inner resources. I felt a surge of confidence and resolve like that I had experienced years before when I conquered my fear of lightning [by climbing up a tree during a thunderstorm]. I was free.

[Ibid.]

Abraham Lincoln
(1809-1865)

[v] The Bible is not my Book and Christianity is not my religion.

[unsourced]

[w] My earlier views at the unsoundness of the Christian scheme of salvation and the human origin of the scriptures, have become clearer and stronger with advancing years and I see no reason for thinking I shall ever change them.

[letter to Judge J.S. Wakefield, after the death of Willie Lincoln]

[x] Human nature will not change. In any future great national trials, compared with the men of this, we shall have as weak and as strong, as silly and as wise, as bad and as good.

[Response to a Serenade. 10 November 1864]

[y] You cannot bring about prosperity by discouraging thrift. You cannot strengthen the weak by weakening the strong. You cannot help the wage earner by pulling down the wage payer. You cannot further the brotherhood of man by encouraging class hatred. You cannot help the poor by destroying the rich. You cannot keep out of trouble by spending more than you earn. You cannot build character and courage by taking away man's initiative and industry. You cannot help men permanently by doing for them what they could and should do for themselves.

[1858]

Robert Lindner
(1914-1956)

[z] In the crowd, herd or gang, it is a mass-mind that operates -- which is to say, a mind without subtlety, a mind without compassion, a

mind, finally, uncivilized.

[Must You Conform?, 1956]

John Locke
(1632-1704)

[a] Faith is the assent to any proposition not made out by the deduction of reason but upon the credit of the proposer.

[An Essay Concerning
Human Understanding, 1690]

[b] Things then are good or evil, only in reference to pleasure or pain. That we call good, which is apt to cause or increase pleasure, or diminish pain in us; or else to procure or preserve us the possession of any other good or absence of any evil. And, on the contrary, we name that evil which is apt to produce or increase any pain, or diminish any pleasure in us: or else to procure us any evil, or deprive us of any good.

[Human Understanding,
Book 2: Ch. 20]

Cesare Lombroso
(1836-1909)

[c] The ignorant man always adores what he cannot understand.

[The Man of Genius. Part III, Chap. 3]

Jack London
(1876-1916)

[d] Do you know the only value human life has is what life puts upon itself?

[The Sea-Wolf]

[e] I see the soul as nothing else than the sum of activities of the organism plus personal habits -- plus inherited habits, memories, experiences, of the organism. I believe that when I am dead, I am dead. I believe that with my death I am just as much obliterated as the last mosquito you and I squashed.

[unsourced]

Erich Friedrich Wilhelm Ludendorff
(1865-1937)

[f] I decline Christianity because it is Jewish, because it is international and because, in cowardly fashion, it preaches peace on Earth.

[Deutsche Gottesglaube]

Martin Luther
(1483-1546)

[g] Reason should be destroyed in all Christians.

[unsourced]

Thomas Babington,
Lord Macaulay
(1800-1859)

[h] The Puritans hated bear-baiting, not because it gave pain to the bear, but because it gave pleasure to the spectators.

[History of England. Chap. 2]

[i] The Church is the handmaid of tyranny and the steady enemy of liberty.

[unsourced]

Arthur Machen
(1863-1947)

[j] It was better he thought, to fail in attempting exquisite things than to succeed in the department of the utterly contemptible.

[The Hill of Dreams. Chap. 5]

Niccolo Machiavelli
(1469-1527)

[k] An armed republic submits less easily to the rule of one of its citizens than a republic armed by foreign forces. Rome and Sparta were for many centuries well armed and free. The Swiss are well armed and enjoy great freedom. For among other evils caused by

being disarmed, it renders you contemptible. It is not reasonable to suppose that one who is armed will obey willingly one who is unarmed; or that any unarmed man will remain safe among armed servants.

[The Prince]

[l] ...The answer is that one would like to be both the one and the other; but because it is difficult to combine them, it is far better to be feared than loved if you cannot be both. ...Men worry less about doing an injury to one who makes himself loved than to one who makes himself feared. The bond of love is one which men, wretched creatures that they are, break when it is to their advantage to do so; but fear is strengthened by a dread of punishment which is always effective.

[Ibid.]

[m] You must understand, therefore, that there are two ways of fighting: by law or by force. The first way is natural to men, and the second to beasts. But as the first way often proves inadequate one must needs have recourse to the second.

[Ibid.]

[n] Any man who tries to be good all the time is bound to come into ruin among the great number who are not good. Hence a prince who wants to keep his authority must learn how not to be good, and use that knowledge, or refrain from using it, as necessity requires.

[Ibid.]

Charles Mackay
(1814-1889)

[o] Cannon-balls may aid the truth,
But thought's a weapon stronger;
We'll win our battles by its aid;
         Wait a little longer.

[The Good Time Coming]

[p] How we should pity the arrogance of the worm that crawls at our feet, if we knew that it also desired to know the secrets of futurity, and imagined that meteors shot athwart the sky to warn it that a tom-tit was hovering near

to gobble it up; that storms and earthquakes, the revolutions of empires, or the fall of mighty monarchs, only happened to predict its birth, its progress, and its decay! Not a whit less presuming has man shewn himself; not a whit less arrogant are the sciences, so called, of astrology, augury, necromancy, geomancy, palmistry, and divination of every kind.

[Extraordinary Popular Delusions And The Madness Of Crowds]

Archibald MacLeish
(1892-1982)

[q] The dissenter is every human being at those moments of his life when he resigns momentarily from the herd and thinks for himself.

["In Praise of Dissent"]

James Madison
(1751-1836)

[r] Religious bondage shackles and debilitates the mind and unfits it for every noble enterprise... During almost fifteen centuries has the legal establishment of Christianity been on trial. What have been its fruits? More or less, in all places, pride and indolence in the clergy; ignorance and servility in laity; in both, superstition, bigotry, and persecution.

[Memorial and Remonstrance Against Religious Assessments]

[s] ...the appropriation of funds of the United States for the use and support of religious societies [is] contrary to the article of the Constitution which declares that "Congress shall make no law respecting a religious establishment."

[veto message, 28 February 1811]

Thomas Malthus
(1766-1834)

[t] A mob, which is generally the growth of a redundant population goaded by resentment for real sufferings, but totally ignorant of the quarter from which they originate, is of all monsters the most fatal to freedom. It fosters a prevailing tyranny and engenders one where it was not; and though in its dreadful fits of

resentment it appears occasionally to devour its unsightly offspring; yet no sooner is the horrid deed committed, than, however unwilling it may be to propagate such a breed, it immediately groans with a new birth.

[An Essay on the Principle of Population...]

Marcus Aurelius Antoninus
(121-180)

[u] A man should be upright, not be kept upright.

[Meditations. III, 5]

[v] Get used to thinking that there is nothing Nature loves so well as to change existing forms and to make new ones like them.

[Ibid. 36]

[w] Be satisfied with success in even the smallest matter, and think that even such a result is no trifle.

[Ibid. IX, 29]

[x] The opinion of 10,000 men is of no value if none of them know anything about the subject.

[unsourced]

Christopher Marlowe
(1564-1593)

[y] I count religion but a childish toy, and hold there is no sin but innocence.

[The Jew Of Malta]

Emma Martin
(1812-1851)

[z] Religion, with an upward glancing eye, asks what there is above. Philosophy looks around her and seeks to make a happy home of earth. Religion asks what God would have her do:--Philosophy, what nature's laws advise. Religion has never given us laws in which cruelty and vice may not be seen, but Philosophy's pure moral code may be thus briefly

stated: Happiness is the great object of human existence....

["A Few Reasons for Renouncing Christianity..."]

[a] It never occurred to my mind, nor did any controversy ever suggest the thought, that possibly the Bible itself might not be what it appeared.

[Ibid.]

[b] The person much inclined to ask God's assistance, learns to repose on the hope of its obtainment, instead of actively seeking the good desired by his own labour.

[Prayer: The Food Of Priestcraft And Bane Of Common Sense]

Harriet Martineau
(1802-1876)

[c] I certainly had no idea how little faith Christians have in their own faith till I saw how ill their courage and temper can stand any attack on it.

[Harriet Martineau's Autobiography]

[d] I certainly never believed, more or less, in the "essential doctrines" of Christianity, which represent God as the predestinator of men to sin and perdition, and Christ as their rescuer from that doom. I never was more or less beguiled by the trickery of language by which the perdition of man is made out to be justice, and his redemption to be mercy.

[Ibid.]

[e] As the astronomer rejoices in new knowledge which compels him to give up the dignity of our globe as the centre, the pride, and even the final cause of the universe, so do those who have escaped from the Christian mythology enjoy their release from the superstition which fails to make them happy, fails to make them good, fails to make them wise, and has become as great an obstacle in the way of progress as the prior mythologies which it took the place of two thousand years ago.

[Ibid.]

Groucho Marx
(1890-1977)

[f] ...a man with an open mind -- you can feel the breeze from here!

[unsourced]

Karl Marx
(1818-1883)

[g] Religion is the sigh of the oppressed creature, the heart of a heartless world, and the soul of soulless conditions. It is the opium of the people.
[A Contribution To The Critique Of Hegel's Philosophy Of Right, 1844]

Daniel Gregory Mason
(1873-1953)

[h] The ideal of Independence requires resistance to the herd spirit now so widespread, to our worship of quantity and indifference to quality, to our unthinking devotion to organization, standardization, propaganda, and advertising.

[Artistic Ideals. Page 3]

Jackie Mason
(1931-   )

[i] Life has no meaning beyond this reality. But people keep searching for excuses. First there was reincarnation. Then refabrication. Now there's theories of life after amoebas, after death, between death, around death. Now you come back as a shirt, as a pair of pants... "What is the meaning of life?" is a stupid question. Life just exists... I see life as a dance. Does a dance have to have a meaning? You're dancing because you enjoy it.

[The Meaning of Life]

Philip Massinger
(1583-1640)

[j] I in mine own house am an emperor
And will defend what's mine.
[The Roman Actor. Act I, Sc. 2]

Edgar Lee Masters
(1869-1950)

[k] He is sent to school

Little or much, where he imbibes the rule
Of safety first and comfort; in his youth
He joins the church and ends the quest of truth.

[The Great Valley]

W. Somerset Maugham
(1874-1965)

[l] People ask you for criticism, but they only want praise.

[Of Human Bondage]

[m] What mean and cruel things men do for the love of God.

[A Writer's Notebook]

[n] I cannot believe in a God that has neither honor nor common sense.

[The Summing Up]

[o] There is no explanation for evil. It must be looked upon as a necessary part of the order of the universe. To ignore it is childish, to bewail it senseless.

[Ibid.]

[p] What does democracy come down to? The persuasive power of slogans invented by wily self-seeking politicians.

[Christmas Holiday]

[q] Through the history of the world there have always been exploiters and exploited. There always will be ... because the great mass of men are made by nature to be slaves, they are unfit to control themselves, and for their own good need masters.

[Ibid.]

Joseph McCabe
(1867-1955)

[r] I once met a pompous ass of a believer who had this religious-sense theory in an exaggerated degree. It is not at all my custom to obtrude the question of religion in conversation, but somebody maliciously tried to draw

the man into debate about God with me. He would say nothing but, with comic solemnity: "I know there is a God." He would not explain further, but his meaning was clear. He felt it. He sensed it. And there is but one possible form in which he could have given precise expression to his actual experience. He was visibly annoyed, but still silent, when I put it. It is: "I have a strong conviction that God exists."

[The Psychology of Religion]

Ian McKellen
(1939-   )

[s] Well, I've often thought the Bible should have a disclaimer in the front saying this is fiction.

[Today, 17 May 2006]

Herman Melville
(1819-1891)

[t] Better sleep with a sober cannibal that a drunken Christian.

[unsourced]

[u] I'll try a pagan friend, thought I, since Christian kindness has turned out to be hollow courtesy.

[Moby Dick]

[v] I baptize you not in the name of the father, but in the name of the Devil. (Ego baptizo te in nomine patris, sed in nomine diaboli.)

[Ibid.]

H.L. Mencken
(1880-1956)

[w] All professional philosophers tend to assume that common sense means the mental habit of the common man. Nothing could be further from the mark. The common man is chiefly to be distinguished by his plentiful lack of common sense: he believes things on evidence that is too scanty, or that distorts the plain facts, or that is full of non sequiturs. Common

sense really involves making full use of all the demonstrable evidence -- and of nothing but the demonstrable evidence.

[Minority Report, H.L. Mencken's Notebooks]

[x] The scientist who yields anything to theology, however slight, is yielding to ignorance and false pretenses, and as certainly as if he granted that a horse-hair put into a bottle of water will turn into a snake.

[Ibid.]

[y] The fact that I have no remedy for all the sorrows of the world is no reason for my accepting yours. It simply supports the strong probability that yours is a fake.

[Ibid.]

[z] The believing mind is externally impervious to evidence. The most that can be accomplished with it is to induce it to substitute one delusion for another. It rejects all overt evidence as wicked...

[Ibid.]

[a] Under democracy one party always devotes its chief energies to trying to prove that the other party is unfit to rule -- and both commonly succeed, and are right... The United States has never developed an aristocracy really disinterested or an intelligentsia really intelligent. Its history is simply a record of vacillations between two gangs of frauds.

[Ibid.]

[b] Every contribution to human progress on record has been made by some individual who differed sharply from the general, and was thus, almost ipso facto, superior to the general... Such exceptional individuals should be permitted, it seems to me, to enjoy every advantage that goes with their superiority, even when enjoying it deprives the general. They alone are of any significance to history. The rest are as negligible as the race of cockroaches, who have gone unchanged for a million years...

[Ibid.]

[c] What I got in Sunday-School... was simply a firm conviction that the Christian faith was full of palpable absurdities, and the Christian God preposterous... The act of worship, as

carried on by Christians, seems to me to be debasing rather than ennobling. It involves groveling before a Being, who, if He really exists, deserves to be denounced rather than respected.

[from On The Meaning of Life, by Durant]

[d] There is, in fact, no reason to believe that any given natural phenomenon, however marvelous it may seem today, will remain forever inexplicable. Soon or later the laws governing the production of life itself will be discovered in the laboratory, and man may set up business as a creator on his own account. The thing, indeed, is not only conceivable; it is even highly probable.

[1930]

[e] Faith may be defined briefly as an illogical belief in the occurrence of the improbable... A man full of faith is simply one who has lost (or never had) the capacity for clear and realistic thought. He is not a mere ass: he is actually ill.

[New York Times Magazine, 11 September 1955]

[f] The truly civilized man, it seems to me, has already got away from the old puerile demand for a "meaning in life." It needs no meaning to be interesting to him. His satisfactions come, not out of childish confidence that some vague and gaseous god, hidden away in some impossible sky, made him for a lofty purpose and will preserve him to fulfill it, but out of a delight in the operations in the universe about him and of his own mind.

[Treatise on the Gods]

[g] If the theological answer to all questions had ever actually prevailed in the world the progress of the race would have come to an end, and there would be no difference today between a good European and a good pygmy in the African jungles. Everything that we are we owe to Satan and his bootleg apples.

[Ibid.]

[h] The great majority of believers... probably do not know precisely what they believe, but the general cast of their thought is still towards belief.

[Ibid.]

[i] Christian theology is not only opposed to the scientific spirit; it is opposed to every other form of rational thinking.

[Ibid.]

[j] If we do not learn how to laugh we succumb to the melancholy disease which afflicts the race of viewers-with-alarm.

[A Mencken Chrestomathy]

[k] Immorality: The morality of those who are having a better time.

[Ibid.]

[l] Men become civilized not in proportion to their willingness to believe but in proportion to their readiness to doubt.

[unsourced]

[m] There is, in fact, nothing about religious opinions that entitles them to any more respect than other opinions get. On the contrary, they tend to be noticeably silly. If you doubt it, then ask any pious fellow of your acquaintance to put what he believes into the form of an affidavit, and see how it reads.... "I, John Doe, being duly sworn, do say that I believe that, at death, I shall turn into a vertebrate without substance, having neither weight, extent nor mass, but with all the intellectual powers and bodily sensations of an ordinary mammal;... and that, for the high crime and misdemeanor of having kissed my sister-in-law behind the door, with evil intent, I shall be boiled in molten sulphur for one billion calendar years."

[unsourced]

[n] Half the time of all medical men is wasted keeping life in human wrecks who have no more intelligible reason for hanging on than a cow has for giving milk.

[unsourced]

[o] The fact is that the average man's love of liberty is nine-tenths imaginary, exactly like his love of sense, justice and truth. He is not actually happy when free; he is uncomfortable, a bit alarmed, and intolerably lonely. Liberty is not a thing for the great masses of men. It is the exclusive possession of a small and disreputable minority, like knowledge, cour-

age and honor. It takes a special sort of man to understand and enjoy liberty -- and he is usually an outlaw in democratic societies.

[Baltimore Evening Sun, 12 February 1923]

[p] If he [a politician] is a smart and enterprising fellow, which he usually is, he quickly discovers that hooey pleases the boobs a great deal more than sense. Indeed, he finds that sense really disquiets and alarms them -- that it makes them, at best, intolerably uncomfortable, just as a tight collar makes them uncomfortable, or a speck of dust in the eye, or the thought of Hell. The truth, to the overwhelming majority of mankind, is indistinguishable from a headache.

[unsourced]

[q] There is only one honest impulse at the bottom of Puritanism, and that is the impulse to punish the man with a superior capacity for happiness... And there is only one sound argument for democracy, and that is the argument that it is a crime for any man to hold himself out as better than other men, and, above all, a most heinous offense for him to prove it.

[unsourced]

[r] All persons who devote themselves to forcing virtue on their fellow men deserve nothing better than kicks in the pants.

[unsourced]

George Meredith
(1828-1909)

[s] When I was quite a boy I had a spasm of religion which lasted six weeks... But I never since have swallowed the Christian fable.

[unsourced]

[t] The man who has no mind of his own lends it to the priests.

[Fortnightly Review]

John Stuart Mill
(1806-1873)

[u] To question all things; -- never to turn away from any difficulty; to accept no doctrine either from ourselves or from other

people without a rigid scrutiny by negative criticism; letting no facally, or incoherence, or confusion of thought, step by unperceived; above all, to insist upon having the meaning of a word clearly understood before using it, and the meaning of a proposition before assenting to it; -- these are the lessons we learn from ancient dialecticians.

[Inaugural Address as Rector, University of St. Andrew, 1 February 1867]

Kenneth R. Miller
(1948-   )

[v] The American creationist movement has entirely bypassed the scientific forum and has concentrated instead on political lobbying and on taking its case to a fair-minded electorate... The reason for this strategy is overwhelmingly apparent: no scientific case can be made for the theories they advance.

[Science And Creationism, 1984]

[w] The fact of the matter is that the fossil record not only documents evolution, but that it was the fossil record itself which forced natural scientists to abandon their idea of the fixity of species and look instead for a plausible mechanism of change, a mechanism of evolution. The fossil record not only demonstrates evolution in extravagant detail, but it dashes all claims of the scientific creationists concerning the origin of living organisms.

[Ibid.]

Henry Hart Milman
(1791-1868)

[x] Christianity disdained that its God and its Redeemer should be less magnificently honored than the demons (gods) of Paganism. In the service it delighted to breathe, as it were, a sublimer sense into the common appellations of the Pagan worship, whether from the ordinary ceremonial or the more secret mysteries. The church became a temple; the table of the communion an altar, the celebration of the Eucharist, the appalling, or unbloody sacrifice.... The incense, the garlands, the lamps, all were gradually adopted by zealous rivalry, or seized as the lawful spoils of vanquished Paganism and consecrated to the service of Christ.

[History of Christianity,
Vol. III]

A. A. Milne
(1882-1956)

[y] The Old Testament is responsible for more atheism, agnosticism, disbelief -- call it what you will -- than any book ever written; it has emptied more churches than all the counterattractions of cinema, motor bicycle and golf course.

[unsourced]

John Milton
(1608-1674)

[z] High on a Throne of Royal State, which far
Outshone the wealth of Ormus and of Ind,
On where the gorgeous East with richest hand
Show'rs on her Kings Barbaric Pearl and Gold,
Satan exalted sat, by merit rais'd
To that bad eminence.

[Paradise Lost]

[a] To be weak is miserable, doing or suffering.

[Ibid. Book I, Line 157]

[b] Better to reign in hell than serve in heaven.

[Ibid. Line 263]

[c] Black it stood as night,
Fierce as ten furies, terrible as hell,
And shook a dreadful dart; what seem'd his head
The likeness of a kingly crown had on.
Satan was now at hand.

[Ibid. Book II, Line 670]

[d] All hell broke loose.

[Ibid. Book IV, Line 918]

Michel de Montaigne
(1533-1592)

[e] It is not without good reason said, that he

who has not a good memory should never take upon him the trade of lying.

> [Works. Book I,
> Chap. 9. Of Liars]

[f] The laws of conscience, which we pretend to be derived from nature, proceed from custom.

> [Ibid.
> Chap. 22. Of Custom]

[g] A wise man never loses anything if he have himself.

> [Ibid.
> Chap. 38. Of Solitude]

[h] When I play with my cat, who knows whether I do not make her more sport than she makes me?

> [Ibid. Book II,
> Chap. 12. Apology for Ratimond Sebond]

[i] Nature has presented us with a large faculty of entertaining ourselves alone; and often calls us to it, to teach us that we owe ourselves partly to society, but chiefly and mostly to ourselves.

> [Ibid.
> Chap. 18. On Giving the Lie]

[j] Let us permit Nature to take her own way; she better understands her own affairs than we.

> [Ibid. Book III,
> Chap. 13. Of Experience]

[k] Men of simple understanding, little inquisitive and little instructed, make good Christians.

> [Essays]

Joel Moody
(?-?)

[l] Men of generous culture or of great learning, and women of eminent piety and virtue, from the humble cottage to the throne, have been led out for matters of conscience and butchered before a mad rabble lusting after

God. The limbs of men and women have been torn from their bodies, their eyes gouged out, their flesh mangled and slowly roasted, their children barbarously tortured before their eyes, because of religious opinion.

[Science of Evil: First Principles of Human Action]

Charles Leonard Moore
(1854-1923)

[m] And now for what comes next
Thou waitest in thine invulnerable West,
Blazoning more large thy living-lettered text,
"Chance and the tools to those who use them best."

[To America]

Christopher Morley
(1890-1957)

[n] Truth, like milk, arrives in the dark but even so, wise dogs don't bark, only mongrels make it hard for the milkman to come up the yard.

[Dogs Don't Bark at the Milkman]

John, Viscount Morley
(1838-1923)

[o] Evolution is not a force but a process, not a cause but a law.

[On Compromise]

[p] You have not converted a man because you have silenced him.

[Ibid.]

[q] Where it is a duty to worship the sun it is pretty sure to be a crime to examine the laws of heat.

[Voltaire]

Lance Morrow
(?-?)

[r] If you scratch any aggressive tribalism, or nationalism, you usually find beneath its

surface a religious core, some older binding energy of belief or superstition... that is capable of transforming itself into a death-force, with the peculiar annihilating energies of belief...

["In The Name of God,"
Time, 15 March 1993]

**Bill Moyers
(1934-   )**

[s] ...if you believe in the virgin birth of Jesus, his crucifixion and resurrection, and the depiction of the Great Judgment at the end times you must also believe that God is sadistic, brutal, vengeful, callow, cruel and savage -- that God slaughters.

[9/11 And The Sport Of God,
TomPaine.com,
9 September 2005]

**Michael Moynihan
(1969-   )**

[t] Blood can be seen as LIFE, and at the same time it can be equated to DEATH. It is essential to violence in almost all instances. It has powerful sexual connections. It is the key fluid of history, both in terms of where and why it has been shed but as importantly in terms of the genetic information that it potentially carries. And all of these elements or facets of its importance are intrinsically linked and often times mutually dependent.

[interview from The Fifth Path.
Issue Three,
Spring 1992)

[u] If one knows what one wants and has that will fully integrated into their being then there really isn't a choice about what paths to take, nor is there a looming conscience above. I don't see it in terms of good and evil at all, although I do think there are such things as right and wrong in a pragmatic sense. To me morality is something completely operative, but that isn't an excuse for "Anything goes; nothing bothers me" which is a position for dogs. Most people seem to truly believe that they are exercising some kind of control over their lives with such justification, though I think

they are the most cowardly victims of all.

[Ibid.]

[v] There are a lot of things I care about, but I choose what I'm going to care about and I choose things that are actually important and real to me, whereas... [some] people "care" about things that are not real to them and have no bearing on their life whatsoever. It's a bizarre form of masochism.

[interview from The First Stone.
Issue 5, Spring/Summer 1999]

[w] [Some] ...are disturbed when they see that there are actually people that live according to rules that are different to theirs, and people who do live with some sense of aesthetics and order. Those principles have become so anomalous in the present, modern world that they see that as a threat...

[Ibid.]

[x] The only place you will find an ordered society is where people with common background and common interests exist on a more tribal (and by that I do not mean "primitive") level. This is very rare nowadays, certainly so in this polyglot empire of losers we're currently stuck with. The only chance for an ordered society is either for the present one to break down entirely and something more like what I just referred to arise from its ashes, or else the imposition of a dictatorship using tactics of mass-coercion that would make the Third Reich look like a Sunday picnic! But really the question you need to consider is: ordered for WHOM, and for what PURPOSE?

[interview from Not Like Most. Issue 4]

Madalyn Murray (O'Hair)
(1919-1995)

[y] I'm thrilled to feel that I can rely on myself totally and absolutely; that my children are being brought up so that when they meet a problem they can't cop out by foisting it off on God. Madalyn Murray's going to solve her own problems, and nobody's going to intervene. It's about time the world got up off its knees and looked at itself in the mirror and said: "Well, we are men. Let's start acting like it."

[Playboy Interview,
October, 1965]

Mutsuhito, Emperor of Japan
(1852-1912)

[z] Be ever careful in your choices of friends, and let your special love be given to those whose strength of character may prove the whip that drives you ever to fair Wisdom's goal.

[Wisdom's Goal (tr. Arthur Lloyd)]

**Vladimir Nabokov
(1899-1977)**

[a] No free man needs a God.

[Pale Fire]

**Peggy Nadramia
(?-   )**

[b] We [The Church of Satan] are the first group of people in human history who have come together under that title [Satanism] and taken it for ourselves; we are the archivists of Satanic history and the caretakers of Satanic philosophy, and we will not have others defining, delimiting or categorizing Satanists or Satanism.

[addendum to Bob Larson interview
from The Black Flame. Vol. 5, #s 1 & 2]

[c] ...it is the Satanist's purpose to facilitate peace in his own life, and to accomplish this there must be true social order among men, one brought about by removing the restraints on natural conditions such as stratification, and justice. The real "social decay" we all have to deal with was brought about by Christian egalitarianism and its secular sister, humanism.

[Ibid.]

Magister Nemo
(?-   )

[d] As Satanists, we have discovered the value of defiance as an emotional tool to divide ourselves from the herd of humanity which passively moves toward the slaughterhouse. We do not work to endure an average life of tortured guilt, frustration and boredom. We defy these anti-human limitations and recognize that "eternal vigilance is the price of freedom." Defiance is the alarm clock which allows us to keep this vigil.
["SHEMHAMFORASH! The Value of Defiance"]

[e] Satanism is a religion based upon doubt, not faith or belief. A Satanist doubts that there is life after death because there is no proof for it. Belief is not knowledge.
["Satanism and Life After Death"]

Richard Lewis Nettleship
(1846-1892)

[f] It is literally true that this world is everything to us, if only we choose to make it so, if only we "live in the present" because it is eternity.
[Lectures and Memories. I, 72]

Friedrich Nietzsche
(1844-1900)

[g] Christianity has done its utmost to close the circle and declared even doubt to be sin. One is supposed to be cast into belief without reason, by a miracle, and from then on to swim in it as in the brightest and least ambiguous of elements: even a glance towards land, even the thought that one perhaps exists for something else as well as swimming, even the slightest impulse of our amphibious nature - is sin! And notice that all this means that the foundation of belief and all reflection on its origin is likewise excluded as sinful. What is wanted are blindness and intoxication and an eternal song over the waves in which reason has drowned.
[Daybreak]

[h] Even today many educated people think

that the victory of Christianity over Greek philosophy is a proof of the superior truth of the former -- although in this case it was only the coarser and more violent that conquered the more spiritual and delicate. So far as superior truth is concerned, it is enough to observe that the awakening sciences have allied themselves point by point with the philosophy of Epicurus, but point by point rejected Christianity.

[Human, All Too Human]

[i] People to whom their daily life appears too empty and monotonous easily grow religious; this is comprehensible and excusable, only they have no right to demand religious sentiments from those whose daily life is not empty and monotonous.

[Ibid.]

[j] What is new, however, is always evil, being that which wants to conquer and overthrow the old boundary markers and the old pieties; and only what is old is good. The good men are in all ages those who dig the old thoughts, digging deep and getting them to bear fruit -- the farmers of the spirit. But eventually all land is depleted, and the ploughshare of evil must come again and again.

[The Gay Science]

[k] The most senile thing ever thought about man is contained in the celebrated saying 'the ego is always hateful'; the most childish is the even more celebrated 'love thy neighbor as thyself.' -- In the former, knowledge of human nature has ceased, in the latter it has not yet even begun.

[Assorted Opinions
and Maxims]

[l] My idea is that every specific body strives to become master over all space and to extend its force (--its will to power:) and to thrust back all that resists its extension. But it continually encounters similar efforts on the part of other bodies and ends by coming to an arrangement ("union") with those of them that are sufficiently related to it: thus they then conspire together for power. And the process goes on--
[The Will To Power]

[m] Have you noticed there are no interesting people in heaven? -- Just a hint to the girls as to

where they can find their salvation.

[Ibid.]

[n] Behold, I teach you the overman. The overman is the meaning of the earth. Let your will say: the overman shall be the meaning of the earth! I beseech you, my brothers, remain faithful to the earth, and do not believe those who speak to you of otherworldly hopes! Poison-mixers are they, whether they know it or not. Despisers of life are they, decaying and poisoned themselves, of whom the earth is weary: so let them go.

[Thus Spoke Zarathustra]

[o] The earth is full of the superfluous, life has been corrupted by the many-too-many. Let them be lured by "eternal life" out of this life!

[Ibid.]

[p] This is hardest of all: to close the open hand out of love, and keep modest as a giver.

[Ibid. Part II, Chap. 23]

[q] If ye would go up high, then use your own legs! Do not get yourselves carried aloft; do not seat yourselves on other people's backs and heads!

[Ibid. Chap. 73, 10]

[r] The broad effects which can be obtained by punishment in man and beast, are the increase of fear, the sharpening of the sense of cunning, the mastery of the desires; so it is that punishment tames man, but does not make him "better."

[Genealogy of Morals. Second Essay, Aphorism 15]

[s] The sick are the greatest danger for the healthy; it is not from the strongest that harm comes to the strong, but from the weakest.

[Ibid. Third Essay, Aphorism 14]

[t] Two great European narcotics: alcohol and Christianity.

[Ibid. Things the Germans Lack, 2]

[u] The weak and ill-constituted shall perish: first principle of our philanthropy. And one shall help them to do so. What is more harmful

than any vice? Active sympathy for the ill-constituted and weak -- Christianity...

[The Antichrist]

[v] One does well to put on gloves when reading the New Testament. The proximity of so much uncleanliness almost forces one to do this.

[Ibid.]

[w] In Christianity neither morality nor religion come into contact with reality at any point.

[Ibid.]

[x] I condemn Christianity. I raise against the Christian church the most terrible of all accusations that any accuser ever uttered. It is to me the highest of all conceivable corruptions. It has had the will to the last corruption that it even possible. The Christian church has left nothing untouched by its corruption; it has turned every value into an un-value, every truth into a lie, every integrity into a vileness of the soul. Let anyone dare to speak to me of its "humanitarian" blessings! To abolish any distress ran counter to its deepest advantages: it lived on distress, it created distress to externalize itself.

[Ibid.]

[y] I call Christianity the one great curse, the one enormous and innermost perversion... I call it the one immortal blemish of mankind.

[Ibid. Aphorism 62]

[z] No one can draw more out of things, books included, than he already knows. A man has no ears for that to which experience has given him no access.

[Ecce Homo]

[a] God is a gross answer, an indelicacy against us thinkers -- at bottom merely a gross prohibition for us: you shall not think!

[Ibid.]

[b] Every individual may be regarded as representing the ascending or descending line of life. When one has decided which, one has thereby decided a canon for the value of his

egoism. If he represents the ascending line his value is in fact extraordinary -- and for the sake of his life-collective, which with him takes a step forward, the care expended on his preservation, may even be extreme. ...If he represents the descending development, decay, chronic degeneration, sickening... then he can be accorded little value.

[Twilight of the Idols]

[c] The Christian faith is from the beginning sacrifice: sacrifice of all freedom, all price, all self-confidence of the spirit, at the same time enslavement and self-mockery, and self-mutilation.

[Beyond Good and Evil]

[d] Christianity was from the beginning, essentially and fundamentally, life's nausea and disgust with life, merely concealed behind, masked by, dressed up as, faith in "another" or "better" life.

[The Birth of Tragedy]

[e] A certain sense of cruelty towards oneself and others is Christian; hatred of those who think differently; the will to persecute. Mortal hostility against the masters of the earth, against the "noble," that is also Christian. Hatred of mind, of pride, courage, freedom, libertinage of mind, is Christian; hatred of the sense, of the joy of the senses, of joy in general is Christian.

[unsourced]

Robert Nisbet
(1913-1996)

[f] Inequality is the essence of the social bond. The vast range of temperaments, minds, motivations, strengths, and desires that exists in any population is nothing if not the stuff of hierarchy.

[The Twilight of Authority]

Charles Eliot Norton
(1827-1908)

[g] The loss of religious faith among the most civilized portion of the race is a step from childishness toward maturity.
[letter to Goldwin Smith, 14 June 1897]

Mary Flannery O'Connor
(1925-1964)

[h] I'm going to preach there was no Fall because there was nothing to fall from, and no Redemption because there was no Fall, and no Judgment because there wasn't the first two. Nothing matters but that Jesus was a liar.

[Wise Blood]

J. Robert Oppenheimer
(1904-1967)

[i] There must be no barriers to freedom of inquiry. There is no place for dogma in science. The scientist is free, and must be free to ask any question, to doubt any assertion, to seek for any evidence, to correct any errors.

[Life, 10 October 1949]

[j] As long as men are free to ask what they must, free to say what they think, free to think what they will, freedom can never be lost, and science can never regress.

[Ibid.]

George Orwell
(1903-1950)

[k] We are all capable of believing things which we know to be untrue. And then, when we are finally proved wrong, impudently twisting the facts so as to show that we were right. Intellectually, it is possible to carry on this process for an indefinite time: the only check on it is that sooner or later a false belief bumps up against solid reality, usually on a battlefield.

[In Front Of Your Nose]

[l] One must choose between God and Man...

[Orwell Reader]

[m] No doubt alcohol, tobacco, and so forth, are things that a saint must avoid, but sainthood is also a thing that human beings must avoid... Many people genuinely do not wish to be saints, and it is probable that some who achieve or aspire to sainthood have never felt much temptation to be human beings.

[Shooting an Elephant]

Ouida
(1839-1908)

[n] Christianity has ever been the enemy of human love.

[The Failure of Christianity]

[o] The radical defect in Christianity is that it tried to win the world by a bribe, and it has become a nullity.

[Ibid.]

Thomas Paine
(1737-1809)

[p] ...but the Bible is such a book of lies and contradictions there is no knowing which part to believe or whether any...

[The Age of Reason]

[q] The most detestable wickedness, the most horrid cruelties, and the greatest miseries that have afflicted the human race have had their origin in this thing called revelation, or revealed religion. It has been the most destructive to the peace of man since man began to exist. Among the most detestable villains in history, you could not find one worse than Moses, who gave an order to butcher the boys, to massacre the mothers and then rape the daughters. One of the most horrible atrocities found in the literature of any nation.

[Ibid.]

[r] All natural institutions of churches, whether Jewish, Christian, or Turkish, appear to me no other than human inventions, set up to terrify and enslave mankind, and monopolize power and profit.

[Ibid.]

[s] Loving of enemies is another dogma of feigned morality, and has beside no meaning... Those who preach the doctrine of loving their enemies are in general the greatest prosecutors, and they act consistently by so doing; for the doctrine is hypocritical, and it is

natural that hypocrisy should act the reverse of what it preaches.

[Ibid.]

[t] The age of ignorance commenced with the Christian system.

[Ibid.]

[u] The supposed quietude of a good man allures the ruffian; while on the other hand, arms like laws discourage and keep the invader and the plunderer in awe, and preserve order in the world as well as property.

[Thoughts on Defensive War, 1775]

Matt G. Paradise
(1968-   )

[v] To say that sexual objectification is "wrong" is to say that the act of being attracted physically to another person is also "wrong." It is both hypocritical and projecting, not to mention silly. Whether money is made from it or not, the archetype of the sex object will stand proud as both a testimony to our productive animal nature and a taskmaster to correct the herd's collective denial of pure attraction.

["Let's Hear It For Sexual Objectification"
from Not Like Most. Issue 6]

[w] It seems that some "Satanists" are painfully concerned about what others will think of their religious organization [Church of Satan]. Where does this bleeding-heart and unpragmatic concern for the herd come from? Not from a Satanist's heart. To take the Name of Satan means that some folks aren't going to understand you, and many will even unquestioningly dislike you. Good. They don't deserve to "get it" if they get stuck... [on] the word Satan...

[from Not Like Most. Issue 7]

[x] ...it's startling what a little hype can do. Women are burned at the stake in 17th-century New England on mere suspicion of "witchcraft." A man accused of rape or molestation may as well be guilty, trial or no trial, according to the anti-male types. Everyone who likes Nietzsche is an automatic goose-stepper. And, even in these ostensibly "enlightened" times, the human sheep continue to perceive media-fueled

hearsay as the unquestionable truth. The "popular lie" exponentiated.

["The Gospel of Insecurity" from Not Like Most. Issue 8]

[y] ...we [as human beings] are both benevolent and brutal, and... these forces are indivisible, no matter how many dualistic labels and religious sun-fearing people deceitfully subscribe to. When all other fun fear is shed, the deepest layer of terror is the realization of human nature.

["Rosemary Revisited" from Not Like Most. Issue 8]

[z] When you force anti-human Christian values and impossible to attain moralisms upon kids whose marked intelligence repels them from such a servile and unconditionally accepted mindset, don't be surprised if he/she lashes back in resentment.

["Bangin' In Littleton" from Not Like Most. Issue 9]

[a] Those who have the qualifications to succeed and even excel within their given circumstances and time period simply cannot be given equal consideration with ignorant, lazy and uninspired humans without creating resentment in those who possess great talents and abilities and, at the same time, filling the heads of defective types with delusions of not only unearned adequacy but [unearned] outstanding achievement as well.

["The Satanic Side of the Enlightenment" from Not Like Most. Issue 9]

[b] We [Satanists] are inarguably a race apart, a tribe of critical rebels and explorers of what is truly occult (read: hidden).

["Dating Outside Your Race" from Not Like Most. Issue 10]

[c] We Satanists align with Satanism because it represents who we are, not because it's misguidedly perceived as some self-help program, defense mechanism to shield others (or, more importantly, yourself) from your personal issues or character flaws, or ego booster. You either are of the Alien Elite or you aren't.

["The 'I's Have It!" from Not Like Most. Issue 11]

Adam Parfrey
(1957-   )

[d] Conquering -- or, rather, controlling -- the

beast in man is the raison d'etre of Christianity and its decadent flower, capitalism.

["Latter-Day Lycanthropy" from Apocalypse Culture]

[e] Pod people aspire to a manicured destiny -- soft, serene, controlled, filtering any information that does not impinge on their pre-fab gestalt. Their retreat from reality is tempered with enough minor but manageable worries and decisions to negotiate boredom and furnish the mirage of individual mastery. These narcoleptics find sublimity in a jar of mayonnaise. As a consequence of the atrophy of the survival instinct, the Pod People can only breed monsters.

["G.G. Allin: Portrait of the Enemy"
from Apocalypse Culture]

[f] We must look to the true outsiders and not the would-be insiders for an artist truly capable of effective counter-terror against the insidious mantras of consumerist brainwash.

["Aesthetic Terrorism" from Apocalypse Culture]

Coventry Kersey Dighton Patmore
(1823-1896)

[g] Life is not life at all without delight.

[Victory in Defeat]

[h] Some who do not consider that Christianity has proved a failure, do, nevertheless, hold that it is open to question whether the race, as a race, has been much affected by it, and whether the external and visible evil and good which have come of it do not pretty nearly balance one another.

[Christianity and Progress]

Mark Pauline
(1953-   )

[i] Pranks are a constructed, fabricated attack against the framework of the society. They're like a bursting-out. Society paints us all into a corner and the whole point of pranks is to open the trap door and escape!

[interview in RE/Search: Pranks!]

[j] A prank should have a resonance and a ring to it. It should speak of the higher aspirations of human activity. It should go far beyond the limitations one would expect it to have. That's what pranks are all about: the unexpected -- the element of surprise transposed onto some kind of poignant act.

[Ibid.]

Thomas Percy
(1728-1811)

[k] Everye white will have its blacke,
And everye sweete its sowre.

[Reliques of Ancient English Poetry. Sir Cauline,
Part II, Stanza 1]

Pablo Picasso
(1881-1973)

[l] Art is never chaste, one should keep all innocent buffoons steered well away. People who are not prepared well enough for art should never be allowed near it. Yes, art is dangerous. If it is chaste, it's not art.

[unsourced]

Robert M. Pirsig
(1928-   )

[m] Metaphysics is a restaurant where they give you a thirty-thousand-page menu, and no food.

[Lila: An Inquiry Into Morals]

Plato
(428-348 B.C.E.)

[n] ...Then anyone who leaves behind him a written manual, and likewise anyone who receives it, in the belief that such writing will be clear and certain, must be exceedingly simpleminded...

[Phaedrus]

[o] The man who makes everything that leads

to happiness depend upon himself, and not other men, has adopted the very best plan for living happily.

[unsourced]

Plutarch
(46-120)

[p] We must not treat legend as if it were history.

[Isis & Osiris, 374]

[q] Cato used to assert that wise men profited more by fools, than fools by wise men; for that wise men avoided the faults of fools, but that fools would not imitate the good examples of wise men.

[Lives. Modern Library Giant edition. p. 417]

[r] Knavery is the best defence against a knave.

[Of Bashfulness]

[s] Themistocles being asked whether he would rather be Achilles or Homer, said, "Which would you rather be, -- a conqueror in the Olympic games, or the crier that proclaims who are conquerors?"

[Apophthegms of Kings and Great Commanders. Themistocles]

[t] After he routed Pharnaces Ponticus at the first assault, he wrote thus to his friends: "I came, I saw, I conquered."

[Roman Apophthegms. Caesar]

[u] It is a thing of no great difficulty to raise objections against another man's oration, -- nay, it is a very easy manner; but to produce a better in its place is a work extremely troublesome.

[Of Hearing. 6]

Edgar Allan Poe
(1809-1849)

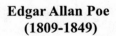

[v] From childhood's hour I have not been
As others were -- I have not seen
As others saw -- I could not bring
My passions from a common spring --
From the same source I have not taken

My sorrow -- I could not awaken
My heart to joy at the same tone --
And all I loved -- I loved alone --
Then -- in my childhood, in the dawn
Of a most stormy life -- was drawn
From every depth of good and ill
The mystery which binds me still...

["Alone"]

Polybius
(200?-118 B.C.E.)

[w] Since the masses of the people are inconstant, full of unruly desires, passionate and reckless of consequence, they must be filled with fears to keep them in order. The ancients did well, therefore, to invent gods, and the belief in punishment after death.

[Histories, ca. 125 B.C.E.]

Alexander Pope
(1688-1744)

[x] Yet let not each gay turn thy rapture move;
For fools admire, but men of sense approve.

[Essay on Criticism. Line 190]

[y] Charms strike the sight, but merit wins the soul.

[The Rape of the Lock.
Canto V, Line 34]

[z] Know then thyself, presume not God to scan
The proper study of mankind is man.

["The Riddle of the World"]

Alan Porter
(1899-1942)

[a] There should between true lovers be an excellent immodesty.

[A Plea That Shame
Be Forgotten]

**Ezra Pound
(1885-1972)**

[b] The act of bellringing is symbolic of all proselytizing religions. It implies the pointless interference with the quiet of other people.

[unsourced]

**Robert M. Price
(1954-   )**

[c] When a group has staked everything on a religious belief, and 'burned their bridges behind them,' only to find this belief disconfirmed by events, they may find disillusionment too painful to endure. They soon come up with some explanatory rationalization, the plausibility of which will be reinforced by the mutual encouragement of fellow-believers in the group. In order to increase further the plausibility of their threatened belief, they may engage in a massive new effort at proselytizing. The more people who can be convinced, the truer it will seem [...] In the final analysis, then, a radical disconfirmation of belief might be just what a religious movement needs to get off the ground!

[Beyond Born Again]

Ayn Rand
(1905-1982)

[d] ...if devotion to truth is the hallmark of morality, then there is no greater, nobler, more heroic form of devotion than the act of a man who assumes the responsibility of thinking.... the alleged short-cut to knowledge, which is faith, is only a short-circuit destroying the mind.

[Atlas Shrugged]

[e] And now I see the face of god, and I raise this god over the earth, this god whom men have sought since men came into being, this god who will grant them joy and peace and pride. This god, this one word: I.

[Anthem]

James Randi
(1928-   )

[f] I hereby state my opinion that the notion of a god is a superstition and that there is no evidence for the existence of any god(s). Further, devils, demons, angels and saints are myths; there is no life after death, no heaven or hell; the Pope is a dangerous, bigoted, medieval dinosaur, and the Holy Ghost is a comic-book character worthy of laughter and derision. I accuse the Christian god of murder by allowing the Holocaust to take place -- not to mention the "ethnic cleansing" presently being performed by Christians in our world -- and I condemn and vilify this mythical deity for encouraging racial prejudice and commanding the degradation of women.

[statement issued to challenge U.S. state blasphemy laws, 1995]

Ragnar Redbeard
(?-?)

[g] Gods are at a discount; devils are in demand.

[Might Is Right]

[h] Although the average man has taken no part in manufacturing moral codes and statute laws, yet how he obeys then with doglike submissiveness. He is trained to obedience, like oxen are broken to the yoke of their masters. He is a born thrall habituated from childhood to be governed by others.

[Ibid.]

[i] Both ancient and modern Christianism and all that has its root therein is the negation of everything grand, noble, generous, heroic, and the glorification of everything feeble, atrocious, dishonorable, dastardly. The cross is now, and ever has been, an escutcheon of shame. It represents a gallows and a Semite slave swinging thereon. For two thousand years it has absolutely overturned human reason, overthrown common sense, infected the world with madness, submissiveness, degeneracy.

[Ibid.]

[j] You may trace Equality in letters of silver on tablets of burnished gold, but without engineering a perpetual miracle, you can not make it -- true.

[Ibid.]

[k] All living beings are pursuing and being pursued. Woe unto those who stumble! Woe unto Ye who fall!

[Ibid.]

[l] Self-preservation first, foremost, above all things and at whatever cost is the law of the jungle. So must it be among human carnivores. So it is, for society is a jungle. Therefore O reader! go forth and win!

[Ibid.]

[m] "Belief" is a war stratagem -- an instrument of deceit, a convenient falsification formula -- a beautiful hoodwink.

[Ibid.]

[n] Right and Wrong, like Up and Down, East and West, are relative terms, without any fixed or finite meaning. What is good for the goose is not always good for the gander. Newfoundland lies East from Chicago, but West from Berlin. All depends upon the point of view. Consequently what may be "right" in one age may in another age be wholly "wrong."

[Ibid.]

[o] O ye generations of Christ-deluded imbeciles! Ye swarms of moonstruck meeklings! Ye burnt out cinders of men! Ye bleeding lambs! One day! One day! Ye shall be flung to the lions! Behold! I spit upon your Idols -- your Opinions. Now would I pour molten hell through the ventricles of your soul.

[Ibid.]

Wilhelm Reich
(1897-1957)

[p] ...full sexual consciousness and a natural regulation of sexual life mean the end of mystical feelings of any kind, that, in other words, natural sexuality is the deadly enemy of mystical religion. The church, by making the fight over sexuality the center of its dogmas and of its influence over the masses, confirms this concept.

[The Mass Psychology
of Fascism]

Salomon Reinach
(1858-1932)

[q] From the literary point of view, the Koran has little merit. Declamation, repetition, puerility, a lack of logic and coherence strike the unprepared reader at every turn. It is humiliating to the human intellect to think that this mediocre literature has been the subject of innumerable commentaries, and that millions of men are still wasting time absorbing it.

[Orpheus: A History of Religion]

John E. Remsberg
(1848-1919)

[r] This doctrine of forgiveness of sin is a premium on crime. "Forgive us our sins" means "Let us continue in our iniquity."... In teaching this doctrine Christ committed a sin for which his death did not atone, and which can never be forgiven.

[The Christ]

[s] The Christ is a myth. The Holy Ghost Priestcraft overshadowed the harlot Superstition; this Christ was born; and the Joseph of humanity, beguiled by the Gabriel of credulity, was induced to support the family. But the soldiers of Reason have crucified the illegitimate impostor, he is dead; and the ignorant disciples and hysterical women who still linger about the cross should take his body down and bury it.

[Ibid.]

Ernest Renan
(1823-1892)

[t] No miracle has ever taken place under conditions which science can accept. Experience shows, without exception, that miracles occur only in times and in countries in which miracles are believed in, and in the presence of persons who are disposed to believe them.

[The Life Of Jesus, 1863]

Jules Renard
(1864-1910)

[u] I don't know if God exists, but it would be better for His reputation if He didn't.

[unsourced]

Boyd Rice
(1956-   )

[v] You can't separate creative force and destructive force, there has to be a balance between them.

[interview from The Fifth Path.

Issue Three, Spring 1992]

[w] Cultivate whatever empowers you personally, whatever minimizes any influence exercised over you by the dominant culture. Weed out whatever hinders you or whatever threatens in any way to subvert your instinct.

[Ibid.]

[x] You can't legislate sanity. There are always going to be people who have a screw loose or have been abused by somebody, and their reaction to that abuse may be overkill. You can't blame it on guns, music, or whatever it is people are trying to blame it on now.

[interview from Lucifer Rising by Gavin Baddeley, p. 239]

[y] All that humankind thinks is great and mighty is but a disease upon life and must be made to perish if life is to continue. That which modern man has worshiped as being grand and noble is but an affliction. All that has given the appearance of granting freedom to mankind, has in fact ordained its enslavement, impairing and crippling from within while outwardly bearing the banner of liberty.

["The End of the World," from Apocalypse Culture]

[z] Love is one of those words whose meaning is seen as absolute and universal, yet there are more varieties of love than there are different factions of Christianity. As most people define it, I'd say it's lust diluted with sentimentality. I have nothing against lust or sentimentality per se, but they aren't a particularly winning combination.

[interview from Answer ME! Number Three]

[a] [Rights are] a figment of the fertile imagination of man. They have to be created by legislation and enforced by punitive "laws," since they exist purely outside the realm of reality. In the final analysis, you have only the rights you take or make -- all else is simply wishful thinking.

[Ibid.]

[b] I have no idea what is meant by the word [equality], since I've never once seen any substantive example of it. Is a strong man equal to a weak man? An intelligent man equal to a congenital idiot? An ugly person equal to a beautiful one? If so, then what

exactly is meant by "equal?" If it makes other people happy to imagine that fifty pounds of lead is equal to fifty pounds of gold, then that's their choice. Personally, I just don't see it.

[Ibid.]

[c] ...the superior man is capable of unimaginable powers of self-transformation. But I would be quick to add that the superior man is also the person least in need of self-transformation, and therefore least likely to pursue it.

["Remembering LaVey" from
The Black Flame. Vol. 6, #s 3 & 4]

[d] The final disposition of any idea, no matter how earthshaking, is always the same. Many will believe it. Still more will speak of it. Few will live it. I say this not as a cynic or gloom-monger, but as a realist.

[Ibid.]

[e] You realize that everything is completely fictional and completely made-up; that it's only real for people because everybody's in agreement... but you don't have to agree... People project those values onto things, but the values aren't in those things. The fact that people are collectively imagining the same values at the same time props up the whole system.

[interview from RE/Search: Pranks!]

[f] What we're talking about is the alchemy of thought. What you think about anything defines how you perceive it, and how you perceive it defines what your experience of it will be. Alter the thought and you've also altered perception and experience.

[Rice as co-interviewer of Barry Alphonso in RE/Search: Pranks!]

[g] In every sense, we create our own reality, and this goes much further than most people are aware of or are willing to admit. The reason most people can't see this is because everyone is creating their own reality, but 99.9% of them are creating the same one -- using the same basic materials: the same beliefs, the same values, the same EVERYTHING. And together it all appears to be one "reality."

[Ibid.]

[h] I see the process of belief as a process of self-deception. Basically it's a vehicle by

which ideas can gain control over people's minds and therefore their lives. Beliefs dictate the precise parameters of people's consciousness of their behavior and perception. A belief paints the world in its own image.

[Ibid.]

Marilla M. Ricker
(1840-1920)

[i] Children should be taught that no amount of so-called religion will compensate for rheumatism; that Christianity has nothing to do with morality; that vicarious atonement is a fraud and a lie; that to be born well and strong is the highest birth; that the Bible is no more inspired than The Philistine; that sin is a transgression of the laws of life; and that the blood of all the bulls and goats and lambs of ancient times, and the blood of Jesus or any other man never had nor can have the least effect in making a life what it would have been had it obeyed the laws of life.

["What Is Prayer?"
The Four Gospels, 1911]

[j] Man has asked for the truth and the Church has given him miracles. He has asked for knowledge, and the Church has given him theology. He has asked for facts, and the Church has given him the Bible. This foolishness should stop. The Church has nothing to give man that has not been in cold storage for two thousand years. Anything would become stale in that time.

[Science Against Creeds, I Am Not Afraid Are You?]

Gene Roddenberry
(1921-1991)

[k] I was born into a supernatural world in which all my people --my family-- usually said "That is because God willed it," or gave other supernatural explanations for whatever happened. When you confront those statements on their own, they just don't make sense. They are clearly wrong. You need a certain amount of proof to accept anything, and that proof was not forthcoming to support those statements.

[unsourced]

[l] We must question the story logic of having an all-knowing all-powerful God, who creates

faulty humans, and then blames them for his own mistakes.

[Free Inquiry, Autumn 1992]

[m] I condemn false prophets, I condemn the effort to take away the power of rational decision, to drain people of their free will -- and a hell of a lot of money in the bargain... For most people, religion is nothing more than a substitute for a malfunctioning brain.

[The Humanist,
March-April 1991]

L.A. Rollins
(?-?)

[n] Morality... is a myth invented to promote the interests / desires / purposes of the inventors. Morality is a device for controlling the gullible with words.

[The Myth of Natural Rights]

Franklin Delano Roosevelt
(1882-1945)

[o] No man can tame a tiger into a kitten by stroking it. There can be no appeasement with ruthlessness. There can be no reasoning with an incendiary bomb.

[fireside chat, 29 December 1940]

Theodore Roosevelt
(1858-1919)

[p] We should encourage rifle practice among schoolboys, and indeed among all classes, as well as in the military services by every means in our power... The first step -- in the direction of preparation to avert war if possible, and to be fit for war if it should come -- is to teach men to shoot!

[last message to Congress]

Michael Rose
(1962-   )

[q] Any social order worth a damn will have a trapezoidal organization. In other words, it will have a small elite at the top, and a broad

and largely undifferentiated mass at the bottom.

["On The Uses of Fascism"]

[r] Support for the Christian agenda is... vastly overestimated. Many might superficially agree with their calls for renewed morality. The difference is that while to the fundamentalist Christian, morality means living strictly in accordance with biblical teachings, to most people it just has a nice sound to it. To the masses it just means that you should wear a Goodguy Badge all the time. They are too busy enjoying their "bread and circuses" -- entitlements and TV -- to worry about the strict biblical asceticism advocated by the fundamentalists.

["The Christians Are Coming!
Or Are They?"]

Jean Jacques Rousseau
(1712-1778)

[s] Christianity preaches only servitude and dependence. Its spirit is so favorable to tyranny that it always profits such a regime. True Christians are made to be slaves, and they know it and do not mind; this short life counts for too little in their eyes.

[The Social Contract]

Salman Rushdie
(1947-   )

[t] The idea of the sacred is quite simply one of the most conservative notions in any culture, because it seeks to turn other ideas --uncertainty, progress, change -- into crimes.

[Is Nothing Sacred?,
Herbert Reade Memorial Lecture,
6 February 1990]

[u] To respect Louis Farrakhan, we must understand, is simply to agree with him... If dissent is now also to be thought of as a form of "dissing," then we have indeed succumbed to the thought police.

[to Reuters News Service,
17 April 1996]

Bertrand Russell
(1872-1970)

[v] William James used to preach the 'will to believe.' For my part, I should wish to preach the 'will to doubt.' ... What is wanted is not the will to believe, but the will to find out, which is the exact opposite.

[Skeptical Essays. 1928]

[w] I wish to propose for the reader's favorable consideration a doctrine which may, I fear, appear wildly paradoxical and subversive. The doctrine in question is this: that it is undesirable to believe a proposition when there is no ground whatever for supposing it true. I must of course admit that if such an opinion became common it would completely transform our social life and our political system; since both are at present faultless, this must weigh against it.

[Ibid.]

[x] We want to stand upon our own feet and look fair and square at the world -- its good facts, its bad facts, its beauties, and its ugliness; see the world as it is and be not afraid of it. Conquer the world by intelligence and not merely by being slavishly subdued by the terror that comes from it.

[Why I Am Not A Christian]

[y] I say quite deliberately that the Christian religion, as organized in its churches, has been and still is the principal enemy of moral progress in the world.

[Ibid.]

[z] There is something feeble and a little contemptible about a man who cannot face the perils of life without the help of comfortable myths. Almost inevitably some part of him is aware that they are myths and that he believes them only because they are comforting. But he dare not face this thought! Moreover, since he is aware, however dimly, that his opinions are not real, he becomes furious when they are disputed.
[Human Society in Ethics and Politics]

[a] So far as I can remember, there is not one

word in the Gospels in praise of intelligence.

["Has Religion Made Useful Contributions to Civilization?"]

[b] I do not think the existence of the Christian God any more probable than the existence of the Gods of Olympus or Valhalla. To take another illustration: nobody can prove that there is not between Earth and Mars a china teapot revolving in an elliptic orbit, but nobody thinks this sufficiently likely to be taken into account in practice. I think the Christian God just as unlikely.

[unsourced]

[c] We may define "faith" as the firm belief in something for which there is no evidence. Where there is evidence, no one speaks of "faith." We do not speak of faith that two and two are four or that the earth is round. We only speak of faith when we wish to substitute emotion for evidence. The substitution of emotion for evidence is apt to lead to strife, since different groups, substitute different emotions.

[unsourced]

[d] The most intelligent individuals on the average breed least, and do not breed enough to keep their numbers constant. Unless new incentives are discovered to induce them to breed they will soon not be sufficiently numerous to supply the intelligence needed for maintaining a highly technical and elaborate system. Further, we must expect, at any rate, for the next hundred years, that each generation will be congenitally stupider than its predecessor, and we shall gradually become incapable of wielding the science we already have.

[Speech. 1930]

[e] The fact that an opinion has been widely held is no evidence whatever that it is not entirely absurd; indeed, in view of the silliness of the majority of mankind, a widespread belief is more likely to be foolish than sensible.

[Marriage and Morals, 1929]

**Marquis de Sade
(1740-1814)**

[f] Of every country and every government, when will you prefer the science of knowing man to that of shutting him up and killing him?

[Aline et Valcour]

[g] The idea of God is the sole wrong for which I cannot forgive mankind.

[Ibid.]

[h] Imperious, choleric, irascible, extreme in everything, with a dissolute imagination the like of which has never been seen, atheistic to the point of fanaticism, there you have me in a nutshell, and kill me again or take me as I am, for I shall not change.

[Marquis de Sade's Last Will And Testament]

[i] There is no God, Nature sufficeth unto herself; in no wise hath she need of an author.

[Cur-de-fer, in Justine]

[j] ...Anything beyond the limits and grasp of the human mind is either illusion or futility; and because your god having to be one or the other of the 2, in the 1st instance I should be mad to believe in him, and in the 2nd a fool.

[unsourced]

Carl Sagan
(1934-1996)

[k] Finding the occasional straw of truth awash in a great ocean of confusion and bamboozle requires intelligence, vigilance, dedication and courage. But if we don't practice these tough habits of thought, we cannot hope to solve the truly serious problems that face us -- and we risk becoming a nation of suckers, up for grabs by the next charlatan who comes along.

[The Fine Art of Baloney Detection]

[l] The idea that God is an oversized white male with a flowing beard who sits in the sky and tallies the fall of every sparrow is ludicrous. But if by "God" one means the set of physical laws that govern the universe, then clearly there is such a God. This God is emotionally unsatisfying... it does not make much sense to pray to the law of gravity.

[unsourced]

[m] You can't convince a believer of anything; for their belief is not based on evidence, it's based on a deep seated need to believe.

[Contact]

[n] You see, the religious people -- most of them -- really think this planet is an experiment. That's what their beliefs come down to. Some god or other is always fixing and poking, messing around with tradesmen's wives, giving tablets on mountains, commanding you to mutilate your children, telling people what words they can say and what words they can't say, making people feel guilty about enjoying themselves, and like that. Why can't the gods let well enough alone? All this intervention speaks of incompetence. If God didn't want Lot's wife to look back, why didn't he make her obedient, so she'd do what her husband told her? Or if he hadn't made Lot such a shithead, maybe she would have listened to him more. If God is omnipotent and omniscient, why didn't he start the universe out in the first place so it would come out the way he wants? Why's he constantly repairing and complaining? No, there's one thing the Bible makes clear: The biblical God is a sloppy manufacturer. He's not good at design, he's not good at execution. He'd be out of business if there was any competition.

[Ibid.]

Margaret Sanger
(1879-1966)

[o] If Christianity turned the clock of general progress back a thousand years, it turned back the clock two thousand years for woman. Its greatest outrage upon her was to forbid her to control the function of motherhood under any circumstances, thus limiting her life's work to bringing forth and rearing children. Coincident with this, the churchmen deprived her of her place in and before the courts, in the schools, in literature, art and society. They shut from her heart and her mind the knowledge of her love life and her reproductive functions. They chained her to the position into which they had thrust her, so that it is only after centuries of effort that she is even beginning to regain what was wrested from her.

[Woman and the New Race, 1920]

George Santayana
(1863-1952)

[p] Those who cannot remember the past are condemned to repeat it.

[Reason In Common Sense, Life of Reason]

[q] Religious doctrines would do well to withdraw their pretension to be dealing with matters of fact. That pretension is not only the source of the conflicts of religion with science and the vain and bitter controversies of sects...

[Prosaic Misunderstandings, Little Essays]

Siegfried Sassoon
(1886-1967)

[r] I'm amazed at folk drinking the gospels in and never scratching their heads for questions.

[The Old Huntsmen]

Arthur Schnitzler
(1862-1931)

[s] Martyrdom has always been a proof of the intensity, never of the correctness of a belief.
[Buch der Sprüche
und Bedenken]

Arthur Schopenhauer
(1788-1860)

[t] Pride is an established conviction of one's own paramount worth in some particular respect; while vanity is the desire of rousing such a conviction in others. Pride works from within; it is the direct appreciation of oneself. Vanity is the desire to arrive at this appreciation indirectly, from without.

[Essays. Pride]

[u] Princes use God as a kind of bogey with which to frighten grown-up children into bed, if nothing else avails; that's why they attach so much importance to the deity.

["Religion:
A Dialogue"]

[v] Faith and knowledge are related as the scales of a balance; when the one goes up, the other goes down.

[Parerga and Paralipomena]

Olive Schreiner
("Ralph Iron")
(1855-1920)

[w] There's something so beautiful in coming on one's very own inmost thoughts in another. In one way, it's one of the greatest pleasures one has.

[Letter to Havelock Ellis.
March 2, 1885]

Albert Schweitzer
(1875-1965)

[x] The Jesus of Nazareth who came forward publicly as the Messiah, who preached the Kingdom of God, who founded the Kingdom of Heaven upon earth, and died to give his work its final consecration, never had any existence. He is a figure designed by rationalism, endowed with life by liberalism, and clothed by modern theology in an historical garb.

[The Quest of the Historical Jesus]

John Selden
(1584-1654)

[y] The Clergy would have us believe them against our own reason, as the woman would have had her husband against his own eyes, when he took her with another man, which she yet stoutly denied: "What, will you believe your own eyes before your own sweet wife?"

[Table Talk]

Kurt Seligmann
(1900-1962)

[z] Satan is an individualist. He upsets the commandments of Heaven which enforce a definite moral conduct. He inspires us with dreams and hopes. He endows us with bitterness and discontent, but in the end he leads us to the Better...

[Magic, Supernaturalism, and Religion]

Seneca
(4 B.C.E.-65 C.E.)

[a] You roll my log, and I will roll yours.

[Apocolocyntosis. Chap. 9]

[b] It is the characteristic of a weak and diseased mind to fear the unfamiliar.

[Moral Epistles]

[c] Religion is regarded by the common people as true, by the wise as false, and by the rulers as useful.

[quoted by Ira D. Cardiff, What Great Men Think About Religion]

Robert William Service
(1874-1958)

[d] This is the Law of the Yukon; that only the Strong shall thrive;
That surely the Weak shall perish, and only the Fit survive.

[The Law of the Yukon]

William Shakespeare
(1564-1616)

[e] Why, then the world's mine oyster,
Which I with sword will open.
[The Merry Wives of Windsor. Act II, Sc. 2, Line 2]

[f] His worst fault is, he's given to prayer; he is something peevish that way.
[Ibid. Act I, Scene IV]

[g] The weakest kind of fruit drops earliest to the ground.
[The Merchant of Venice.
Act IV, Sc. 1, Line 115]

[h] Thrust your head into the public street, to gaze on Christian fools with varnish'd faces.
[Ibid. Act II, Scene V]

[i] Commit the oldest sins the newest kind of ways.
[King Henry IV. Act IV, Sc. 5, Line 124]

[j] Appetite, a universal wolf.
[Troilus and Cressida. Act I, Sc. 3, Line 121]

[k] Cry "Havoc!" and let slip the dogs of war.
[Julius Caesar. Act III, Sc. 1, Line 273]

[l] This above all: to thine own self be true.
[Hamlet. Act I, Sc. 3, Line 78]

[m] 'Tis now the very witching time of night,
When churchyards yawn and hell itself breathes out
Contagion to this world.
[Ibid. Act III, Sc. 2,
Line 413]

[n] A man may fish with the worm that hath
eat of a king, and eat of the fish that hath fed
of that worm.
[Ibid. Act IV, Sc. 3, Line 29]

[o] The prince of darkness is a gentleman.

[King Lear. Act III,
Sc. 4, Line 147]

[p] Immortal gods, I crave no pelf;
I pray for no man but myself;
Grant I may never prove so fond
To trust man on his oath or bond,
Or a harlot for her weeping,
Or a dog that seems a-sleeping,
Or a keeper with my freedom,
Or my friends if I should need 'em...

[Timon of Athens]

George Bernard Shaw
(1856-1950)

[q] Democracy substitutes selection by the incompetent many for appoint-ment by the corrupt few.

[Major Barbara]

[r] The people who get on in this world are the people who get up and look for the circumstances they want, and, if they can't find them, make them.

[Mrs. Warren's Profession.
Act II]

[s] Do not do unto others as you would they should do unto you. Their tastes may not be the same.

[Man And Superman]

[t] Is the devil to have all the passions as well as all the good tunes?

[Ibid.]

[u] Take care to get what you like, or you will be forced to like what you get.

[Ibid.]

[v] The golden rule is that there are no golden rules.

[Ibid.]

[w] It is not disbelief that is dangerous to our society; it is belief.

[unsourced]

[x] Martyrdom, sir, is what these people like: it is the only way in which a man can become famous without ability.

[The Devil's Disciple,
Act II]

[y] Patriotism is a pernicious, psychopathic form of idiocy.

[unsourced]

Percy Bysshe Shelley
(1792-1822)

[z] There is no God.

["The Necessity of Atheism"]

[a] It is only by hearsay (by word of mouth passed down from generation to generation) that whole peoples adore the God of their fathers and of their priests: authority, confidence, submission and custom with them take the place of conviction or of proofs: they prostrate themselves and pray, because their fathers taught them to prostrate themselves and pray: but why did their fathers fall on their knees?

[Ibid.]

[b] Once, early in the morning, Beelzebub arose,
With care his sweet person adorning,
He put on his Sunday clothes.

[The Devil's Walk,
A Ballad. Stanza 1]

[c] Obedience indeed is only the pitiful and cowardly egotism of him who thinks that he can do something better than reason.
[Queen Mab]

[d] And priests dare babble of a God of
peace,
Even whilst their hands are red with guiltless
blood,
Murdering the while, uprooting every germ

Of truth, exterminating, spoiling all,
Making the earth a slaughter-house!

[Ibid.]

[e] Let Hell unlock
Its mounded Oceans of tempestuous fire...

[Prometheus Unbound]

Marian Noel Sherman, M.D.
(1892-1975)

[f] There is no evidence at all for the existence of a supernatural Supreme
Being. Some people say they know God exists because they feel him in their
hearts. Again that is just childhood conditioning. Others are fond of saying
that there had to be someone, or something to act as a First Cause, but even a
child can see through that argument. If you tell a child "God made the world"
he will usually ask "Then who made God?" If we reply, as the catechism
states, "No one made God. He always was," then why couldn't we just say
that about the world in the first place?

[Toronto Star Weekly, 11 Sept. 1965]

Gene Simmons
(1949-   )

[g] This was always my philosophy -- pragmatism. Let other people go into
trances and think about spirituality... I'd rather concentrate on having something to eat. The here and now. Be glad you can get a good night's sleep and
eat a good meal and, if you're lucky enough, have somebody attractive shar-
ing your bed with you.

[KISS and Make-up]

[h] A crook is about to rob you and points a gun in
your face. Your life is in danger. You could tell
him you love him, try the Jesus path. The same
thing will happen to you that happened to
him. You'll get crucified, and you don't even
have to be a Jew like he was.

[Sex Money Kiss]

[i] When I'm gone, on my tombstone I'd like

'Thank you and goodnight,' because I have no regrets. The sad thing is most people have to check with someone before they do the things that make them happy. We're all passing through; the least we can do is be happy, and the only way to do that is by being selfish.

[unsourced]

George Gaylord Simpson
(1902-1984)

[j] Man stands alone in the universe, a unique product of a long, unconscious, impersonal, material process with unique understanding and potentialities. These he owes to no one but himself, and it is to himself that he is responsible. He is not the creature of uncontrollable and undeterminable forces, but is his own master. He can and must decide and manage his own destiny.

[Life of the Past]

Frank Sinatra
(1915-1998)

[k] When lip service to some mysterious deity permits bestiality on Wednesday and absolution on Sunday, cash me out.

[Interview for Playboy magazine, February 1962]

Elmina D. Slenker
(1827-1908)

[l] When a mere girl, my mother offered me a dollar if I would read the Bible through; ...despairing of reconciling many of its absurd statements with even my childish philosophy, ...I became a sceptic, doubter, and unbeliever, long ere the "Good Book" was ended.

[Studying the Bible, 1870]

Gary Sloan
(?-?)

[m] Their belief in Jesus gives them an indefatigably sympathetic confidant, assuages their fear of death and bereavement, wards off existential angst, assures cosmic purpose, and aligns them with the good guys. So hand-

some are the psychological pay-offs of belief that many, perhaps most, devout orthodox Christians are impervious to all countervailing logic and evidence. Their will to believe vanquishes every disquieting fact, every contrary line of reasoning, no matter how compelling to an impartial eye. Psychologists have a frightening arsenal of terms for the mental habits designed to preserve cherished beliefs: dissociation, absolutist thinking, dichotomization, object permanence, nominal realism, phenomenalistic causality and worse.

["Did Jesus Exist and Does It Matter?"]

Alexander Smith
(1830-1867)

[n] The world is not so much in need of new thoughts as that when thought grows old and worn with usage it should, like current coin, be called in, and, from the mint of genius, reissued fresh and new.

[Dreamthorp.
On The Writing of Essays]

George H. Smith
(1949-   )

[o] Reason is not one tool of thought among many, it is the entire toolbox. To advocate that reason be discarded in some circumstances is to advocate that thinking be discarded - which leaves one in the position of attempting to do a job after throwing away the required instrument.

[Atheism: The Case Against God]

[p] Christianity has nothing to offer a happy man living in a natural, intelligible universe. If Christianity is to gain a motivational foothold, it must declare war on earthly pleasure and happiness, and this, historically, has been its precise course of action. In the eyes of Christianity, man is sinful and helpless in the face of God, and is potential fuel for the flames of hell. Just as Christianity must destroy reason before it can introduce faith, so it must destroy happiness before it can introduce salvation.

[Ibid.]

[q] I am arguing that faith as such, faith as an alleged method of acquiring knowledge, is totally invalid and as a consequence, all

propositions of faith, because they lack rational demonstration, must conflict with reason.

[Ibid.]

[r] Why has Christianity refused, whenever possible, to allow its beliefs to compete in a free marketplace of ideas? The answer is obvious and revealing. Christianity is peddling an inferior product, one that cannot withstand critical investigation. Unable to compete favorably with other theories, it has sought to gain a monopoly through a state franchise...

[Ibid.]

[s] As for Christianity's alleged concern with truth, Christian faith is to free inquiry what the Mafia is to free enterprise. Christianity may be represented as a competitor in the realm of ideas to be considered on the basis of its merits, but this is mere disguise. Like the Mafia, if Christianity fails to defeat its competition by legitimate means (which is a forgone conclusion), it resorts to strong-arm tactics. Have faith or be damned -- this biblical doctrine alone is enough to exclude Christianity from the domain of reason.

[Ibid.]

[t] The leap of faith is a strategic impasse that confronts every Christian in search of converts; and, as he sees the matter, there is no wrong way to become a Christian. It is the end that is important, not the means; it does not matter why you believe, so long as you believe. For the philosopher, in contrast, the paramount issue is the justification of belief, not the fact of belief itself.

[Why Atheism?]

Logan Pearsall Smith
(1865-1946)

[u] There are two things to aim at in life: first, to get what you want; and, after that, to enjoy it. Only the wisest of mankind achieve the second.

[Afterthoughts]

Sydney Smith
(1771-1845)

[v] Preaching has become a by-word for long

and dull conversation of any kind; and whoever wishes to imply, in any piece of writing, the absence of everything agreeable and inviting, calls it a sermon.

[Lady Holland's Memoir. Vol. 1, Chap. 2]

[w] As the French say, there are three sexes,-- men, women, and clergymen.

[Ibid. Chap. 9]

Barbara Smoker
(1923-   )

[x] People who believe in a divine creator, trying to live their lives in obedience to his supposed wishes and in expectation of a supposed eternal reward, are victims of the greatest confidence trick of all time.

["So You Believe in God!" 1974]

[y] To imagine that "God moves in mysterious ways" is to put up a smoke-screen of mystery behind which fantasy may survive in spite of all the facts.

[Ibid.]

[z] Empathizing with the younger children on whom the same confidence trick was being imposed, I embarked on a crusade around the neighbourhood, telling all the kids that there was no Santa Claus. This reached the ears of the father of a neighboring family, who reproved me for spoiling it for the little ones. Spoiling it! I could not understand what he meant. To my mind, they were being made fools of, and I was only saving them from this indignity.

["Why I Am An Atheist"]

Austin Osman Spare
(1888-1956)

[a] I, who enjoy my body with unweary tread, would rather pack with wolves than enter your pest-houses. Sensation... Nutrition... Mastication... Procreation! This is your blind-worm cycle.

[The Anathema of Zos]

[b] I blaspheme your commandments, to pro-

voke and enjoy your bark, your teeth grinding!

[Ibid.]

Herbert Spencer
(1829-1903)

[c] Survival of the fittest.

[First Principles]

[d] We hear with surprise of the savage who, falling down a precipice, ascribes the failure of his foothold to a malicious demon; and we smile at the kindred notion of the ancient Greek, that his death was prevented by a goddess who unfastened for him the thong of the helmet by which his enemy was dragging him. But daily, without surprise, we hear men who describe themselves as saved from shipwreck by "divine interposition"... and the Christian priest who says prayers over a sick man in the expectation that the course of the disease will be stayed, differ only in respect of the agent from whom they expect supernatural aid.

[Ibid.]

[e] The ultimate result of shielding men from the effects of folly is to fill the world with fools.

["State Tamperings with Money Banks"]

[f] Fostering the good-for-nothing at the expense of the good is an extreme cruelty. It is a deliberate storing up of miseries for future generations. There is no greater curse to posterity than that of bequeathing them an increasing population of imbeciles.

[Principles of Sociology]

Oswald Spengler
(1880-1936)

[g] ...There is only one world-outlook that is worthy of us... better a short life, full of deeds and glory, than a long life without content."
[Man and Technics]

[h] World peace... involves the private renunciation of war on the part of the immense

majority, but along with this it involves an unavowed readiness to submit to being the booty of others who do not renounce it.

[The Decline of the West]

Benedictus de Spinoza
(1632-1677)

[i] He who seeks equality between unequals, seeks an absurdity.

[Political Treatise]

Joseph Stalin
(1879-1953)

[j] From each according to his ability, to each according to his work.

[Constitution of the U.S.S.R. (1936). Article 12]

Elizabeth Cady Stanton
(1815-1902)

[k] For fifty years the women of this nation have tried to dam up this deadly stream that poisons all their lives, but thus far they have lacked the insight or courage to follow it back to its source and there strike the blow at the fountain of all tyranny, religious superstition, priestly power, and the canon law.

["The Degraded Status of Woman in the Bible"]

[l] I can say that the happiest period of my life has been since I emerged from the shadows and superstitions of the old theologies, relieved from all gloomy apprehensions of the future, satisfied that as my labors and capacities were limited to this sphere of action, I was responsible for nothing beyond my horizon, as I could neither understand nor change the condition of the unknown world. Giving ourselves, then, no trouble about the future, let us make the most of the present, and fill up our lives with earnest work here.

["The Pleasures of Age." The Boston Investigator, 2 February 1901]

[m] The Bible teaches that woman brought sin and death into the world, that she precipitated the fall of the race, that she was arraigned before the judgment seat of Heaven, tried, condemned and sentenced. Marriage for

her was to be a condition of bondage, maternity a condition of suffering and anguish, and in silence and subjection, she was to play the role of a dependent on man's bounty for all her material wants, and for all the information she might desire.

[unsourced]

Gloria Steinem
(1934-   )

[n] ...we will, I hope, raise our children to believe in human potential, not God...

[Saturday Review of Education, March 1973]

[o] It is an incredible con job when you think of it, to believe something now in exchange for life after death. Even corporations with all their reward systems don't try to make it posthumous.

[unsourced]

George Sterling
(1869-1926)

[p] Thy Banners gleam a little, and are furled;
Against thy turrets surge His phantom tow'rs;
Drugged with his Opiates the nations nod,
Refusing still the beauty of thine hours;
And fragile is thy tenure of this world
Still haunted by the monstrous ghost of God.

["To Science"]

Howard Stern
(1954-   )

[q] Here's what happens when you die -- you sit in a box and get eaten by worms. I guarantee you that when you die, nothing cool happens.
 [Howard Stern Show on E! 12 April 1995]

[r] I don't think there's any difference between the Pope wearing a large hat and parading around with a smoking purse and an

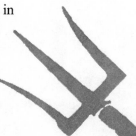

African painting his face white and praying to a rock.

[The Advocate]

Robert Louis Stevenson
(1859-1892)

[s] You cannot run away from a weakness; you must some time fight it out or perish; and if that be so, why not now, and where you stand?

[The Amateur Emigrant]

Sting
(1951-   )

[t] I'm becoming increasingly aware of how self-motivated and self-interested I am. Everybody is, really, but the people who are screwed up are those who won't admit this.

[Every Breath He Takes]

[u] The Catholic Church is full of blood sacrifice and magic, which is probably its attraction. If it were not murky and full of ghostly presences ... it would now be virtually dead. Its appeal lies in its unsettling symbols, its blood-drenched dogmas, and its rule of fear.

[Ibid.]

Harlan F. Stone
(1872-1946)

[v] The law itself is on trial quite as much as the cause which is to be decided.

[U.S. Supreme Court, 1941]

Matthew Stover
(1962-   )

[w] The dark is generous, and it is patient. It is the dark that seeds cruelty into justice, that drips contempt into compassion, that poisons love with grains of doubt. The dark can be patient, because the slightest drop of rain will cause those seeds to sprout. The rain will

come, and the seeds will sprout, for the dark is the soil in which they grow, and it is the clouds above them, and it waits behind the star that gives them light. The dark's patience is infinite. Eventually, even stars burn out.

[Star Wars:
Revenge of the Sith]

Strabo
(ca. 58 B.C.E.-24 C.E.)

[x] The poets were not alone in sanctioning myths, for long before the poets the states and the lawmakers had sanctioned them as a useful expedient.... They needed to control the people by superstitious fears, and these cannot be aroused without myths and marvels.

[Geographia, bk. 1, sct. 2, subsct. 8]

David Levi Strauss
(?-)

[y] In pre-Columbian America, indigenous folklore was dominated by the character of the Trickster. This chief mythological character of the paleolithic world of story, found all over the world in various guises (eventually as "Satan"), was the first prankster.

["The Literature of Pranks"]

Morris Sullivan
(1956-)

[z] Religion -- or at least Christianity -- insists that certain things be considered facts, based purely on faith. In other words, you are supposed to believe, just because the religious view says to. The faithful will tell you, for example, that God exists in fact, in spite of the total lack of empirical evidence for God's existence. If pressed for evidence, they will come up with a series of irrational statements like, "Well, the world couldn't possibly exist unless God made it," or "There has to be a reason for all this to exist." According to the religious world-view, too, all of creation exists for the benefit of man.

["Creationism: Monkeying
With
Science Education"]

William G. Sumner
(1840-1910)

[a] Liberty perishes in all socialistic schemes, and the tendency of such schemes is to the deterioration of society by burdening the good members and relieving the bad ones. The law of survival of the fittest was not made by man and cannot be abrogated by man. We can only, by interfering with it, produce the survival of the unfittest.

[Social Darwinism]

[b] Nature is entirely neutral; she submits to him who most energetically and resolutely assails her. She grants her rewards to the fittest, therefore, without regard to other considerations of any kind.

[Ibid.]

[c] The ignorant, idle, and shiftless have been taught that they are "the people," that the generalities inculcated at the same time about the dignity, wisdom, and virtue of "the people" are true of them, that they have nothing to learn to be wise, but that, as they stand, they possess a kind of infallibility, and that to their "opinion" the wise must bow. It is not cause for wonder if whole sections of these classes have begun to use the powers and wisdom attributed to them for their interests, as they construe them, and to trample on all the excellence which marks civilization as an obsolete superstition.

[Ibid.]

[d] There is a doctrine floating about in our literature that we are born to the inheritance of certain rights. That is another glorious dream, for it would mean that there is something in this world which we got for nothing. But what is the truth? We are born into no right whatever but what has an equivalent and corresponding duty right alongside of it. There is no such thing on this earth as something for nothing.

[Ibid.]

Donald Sutherland
(1934-   )

[e] I'm so far away from believing that it [Heaven] exists, and the only thing I know are jokes about it.
[Inside The Actor's Studio, 13 June 1999]

Algernon Charles Swinburne
(1837-1909)

[f] Man, with a child's pride...
Made God in his likeness, and bowed
Him to worship the Maker he made.

[unsourced]

Thomas Szasz
(1920-   )

[g] History teaches us that persons who make others dependent on them are worshiped, whereas those who help them become independent are disdained or ignored. So long as 'God' is loved and 'Satan' hated, there can be no liberation of the human spirit.

[The Untamed Tongue]

[h] If you talk to God, you are praying; if God talks to you, you have schizophrenia.

[The Second Sin]

Jared Taylor
(1951-   )

[i] If a beggar forces a citizen, under threat of violence, to hand over his money, this is robbery. If government forces the same citizen, under threat or jail, to give money to beggars, this same transfer is called welfare.

[Paved With Good Intentions]

Alfred, Lord Tennyson
(1809-1892)

[j] I built my soul a lordly pleasure-house. Wherein at ease for aye to dwell.

[The Palace of Art. Stanza 1]

[k] For man is man and master of his fate.

[Idylls of the King. Geraint and Enid, I, Line 355]

[l] Blind and naked Ignorance
Delivers brawling judgments, unashamed,
On all things all day long.

[Ibid. Merlin and Vivien, Line 41]

Peter Thorslev
(?-?)

[m] Satan is, after all, an aggressive and inventive spirit, and he thus becomes, I think,

inevitably associated with the aggressive, inventive spirit of man. That proud self-assertion which is also the basis of Romantic and humanist self-reliance.
[The Byronic Hero]

[n] The entire heroic tradition offends not only our sense of realism, but probably also out sense of the democratic, of the commonness of every man.
[Ibid.]

**Thomas Tusser
(1524-1580)**

[o] Naught venture naught have.
[Five Hundred Points of Good Husbandry. October's Abstract]

**Mark Twain
(Samuel Clemens)
(1835-1910)**

[p] I have always felt friendly toward Satan. Of course that is ancestral; it must be in the blood, for I could not have originated it.
[Autobiography of Mark Twain]

[q] The Church has opposed every innovation and discovery from the day of Galileo down to our own time, when the use of anesthetic in childbirth was regarded as a sin because it avoided the biblical curse pronounced against Eve. And every step in astronomy and geology ever taken has been opposed by bigotry and superstition. The Greeks surpassed us in artistic culture and in architecture five hundred years before Christian religion was born.
[from Albert Bigelow Paine;
Mark Twain, a Biography]

[r] It is most difficult to understand the disposition of the Bible God, it is such a confusion of contradictions; of watery instabilities and iron firmnesses; of goody-goody abstract morals made out of words, and concreted hell-born ones made out of acts; of fleeting kindnesses repented of in permanent malignities.
[Letters From
The Earth]

[s] Jealousy. Do not forget it, keep it in mind. It is the key. With it you will come to partly understand God as we go along; without it nobody can understand him. As I have said, he has openly held up this treasonous key himself, for all to see. He says, naively, outspokenly, and without suggestion of embarrassment: "I the Lord thy God am a jealous God." You see, it is only another way of saying, "I the Lord thy God am a small God; a small God, and fretful about small things."

[Ibid.]

[t] Man is a marvelous curiosity... he thinks he is the Creator's pet... he even believes the Creator loves him; has a passion for him; sits up nights to admire him; yes and watch over him and keep him out of trouble. He prays to him and thinks He listens. Isn't it a quaint idea.

[Ibid.]

[u] War talk by men who have been in a war is always interesting; whereas moon talk by a poet who has not been in the moon is likely to be dull.

[Life on the Mississippi. Chap. 45]

[v] The Christian Bible is a drug store. Its contents have remained the same but the medical practice continues. For 1,800 years these changes were slight -- scarcely noticeable... The dull and ignorant physician day and night, and all the days and all the nights, drenched his patient with vast and hideous doses of the most repulsive drugs to be found in the store's stock... He kept him religion sick for eighteen centuries, and allowed him not a well day during all that time.

["Bible Teaching and Religious Practice"]

[w] Of the delights of this world, man cares most for sexual intercourse, yet he has left it out of his heaven.

[unsourced]

[x] If there is a God, he is a malign thug.

[unsourced]

[y] One of the proofs of the immortality of the soul is that myriads have believed it -- they also believed the world was flat.

[Notebook, 1900]

[z] If you can't stand solitude, perhaps others find you boring as well.

[unsourced]

**Carl Van Vechten
(1880-1964)**

[a] The cat, it is well to remember, remains the friend of man because it pleases him to do so and not because he must.

[unsourced]

**Gore Vidal
(1925-   )**

[b] Once people get hung up on theology, they've lost sanity forever. More people have been killed in the name of Jesus Christ than any other name in the history of the world.

[Secular Humanist Bulletin,
Summer 1995]

[c] Christianity is such a silly religion.

[Time, September 28, 1992]

[d] The great unmentionable evil at the centre of our culture is Monotheism. From a barbaric bronze age text known as the Old Testament, three anti-human religions have evolved -- Judaism, Christianity, and Islam. These are sky-god religions. They are patriarchal -- God is the omnipotent father -- hence the loathing of women for 2,000 years in those countries af-

flicted by the sky-god and his male delegates. The sky-god is jealous...

[New Statesman Society, 26 June 1992]

Virgil
(70-19 B.C.E.)

[e] Here's Death, twitching my ear: 'Live' says he, 'for I'm coming.'

[Minor Poems. Copa: Syrisca, a dancing girl, line 38]

Voltaire
(1694-1778)

[f] Christianity is the most ridiculous, the most absurd, and bloody religion that has ever infected the world.

[unsourced]

[g] What can we say to a man who tells you that he would rather obey God than men, and that therefore he is sure to go to heaven for butchering you? Even the law is impotent against these attacks of rage; it is like reading a court decree to a raving maniac. These fellows are certain that the holy spirit with which they are filled is above the law, that their enthusiasm is the only law that they must obey.

[1764]

[h] You will notice that in all disputes between Christians since the birth of the Church, Rome has always favored the doctrine which most completely subjugated the human mind and annihilated reason.

[unsourced]

Kurt Vonnegut, Jr.
(1922-2007)

[i] What the Gospels actually said was: don't kill anyone until you are absolutely sure they aren't well connected.

[Slaughterhouse 5]

[j] How on earth can religious people believe in so much arbitrary, clearly invented balderdash?... The acceptance of a creed, any creed,

entitles the acceptor to membership in the sort of artificial extended family we call a congregation. It is a way to fight loneliness. Any time I see a person fleeing from reason and into religion, I think to myself, There goes a person who simply cannot stand being so goddamned lonely anymore.

[quoted from 2000 Years of Disbelief, Famous People with the Courage to Doubt by James A. Haught]

[k] Say what you will about the sweet miracle of unquestioning faith. I consider a capacity for it terrifying and absolutely vile.

[Mother Night]

[l] I believe that virtuous behavior is trivialized by carrot-and-stick schemes, such as promises of highly improbable rewards or punishments in an improbable afterlife.

[Fates Worse Than Death: An Autobiographical Collage]

**Lois Waisbrooker
(1826-1909)**

[m] Until you let go of God and take hold of yourselves, of the innate powers of your own beings, there is no hope for you. . . . stop praying and go to work.

["The Curse of Godism," ca. 1896]

**Lemuel K. Washburn
(?-?)**

[n] The cross everywhere is a dagger in the heart of liberty.

[Is The Bible Worth Reading
And Other Essays]

[o] Whatever tends to prolong the existence of ignorance or to prevent the recognition of knowledge is dangerous to the well-being of the human race.

[Ibid.]

[p] Our duty to the god of Christianity is to bury him.

[Ibid.]

[q] If man had no knowledge except what he has got out of the Bible he would not know enough to make a shoe.

[Ibid.]

[r] Do not thank God for what man does.

[Ibid.]

[s] An organization that requires the suppression of facts and the discouragement of knowledge in order to maintain its supremacy, is the relic of a tyranny which our free age and our free thought are in duty bound to remove from the earth.

[Ibid.]

[t] The man who gets on his knees has not learned the right use of his legs.

[Ibid.]

[u] The doubter is the safe man; the man who can be depended upon. He does not build upon a foundation of guesswork, and the structure he erects will stand. Let us not fear doubt, but rather fear to have falsehood passed for truth.

[Ibid.]

[v] The church is a bank that is continually receiving deposits but never pays a dividend.

[Ibid.]

[w] Religion is no more the parent of morality than an incubator is the mother of a chicken.

[Ibid.]

[x] What a queer thing is Christian salvation! Believing in firemen will not save a burning house; believing in doctors will not make one well, but believing in a savior saves men. Fudge!

[Ibid.]

George Washington
(1732-1799)

[y] To ensure peace, security, and happiness, the rifle and pistol are equally indispensable.
[Boston Independence Chronicle,
14 January 1790]

[z] The United States is in no way founded

upon the Christian religion.

[Diplomatic message to Malta]

Sir William Watson
(1858-1935)

[a] Lo, with the ancient
Roots of man's nature,
Twines the eternal passion of song.

[England My Mother.
Part II, Stanza 1]

Alan Watts
(1915-1973)

[b] Fanatical believers in the Bible, the Koran and the Torah have fought one another for centuries without realizing that they belong to the same pestiferous club.

[The World's Most
Dangerous Book]

[c] The true believer... if he is somewhat sophisticated, justifies and even glorifies his invincible stupidity as a "leap of faith" or "sacrifice of the intellect."... Such people are, quite literally, idiots -- originally a Greek word meaning an individual so isolated that you can't communicate with him.

[Ibid.]

[d] Today [1973], especially in the United States, there is a taboo against admitting that there are enormous numbers of stupid and ignorant people... Many people never grow up. They stay all their lives with a passionate need for eternal authority and guidance...

[Ibid.]

Herbert George Wells
(1866-1946)

[e] Moral indignation -- jealousy with a halo.
[unsourced]

[f] The greatest evil in the world today is the

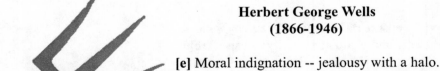

Christian religion.

[unsourced]

[g] I think that it [Christianity] stands for everything most hostile to the mental emancipation and stimulation of mankind. It is the completest, most highly organized system of prejudices and antagonism in existence. Everywhere in the world there are ignorance and prejudice, but the greatest complex of these, with the most extensive prestige and the most intimate entanglement with traditional institutions, is the Roman Catholic Church. It presents many faces to the world, but everywhere it is systematic in its fight against freedom.

[unsourced]

Mae West
(1893-1980)

[h] It's better to be looked over than over looked.

[unsourced]

[i] Women with "pasts" interest men, because men hope history will repeat itself.

[unsourced]

[j] Let men see what's coming to them and women will see what's coming to them.

[unsourced]

[k] I didn't discover curves, I only uncovered them.

[unsourced]

[l] Good women are no fun. The only good woman I can recall is Betsy Ross, and all she ever made was a flag.

[unsourced]

[m] When a girl goes bad, men go right after her.

[unsourced]

[n] Cultivate your curves, they may be dangerous, but they won't be avoided.

[unsourced]

John Hall Wheelock
(1886-1978)

[o] There is a panther caged within my breast,
But what his name there is no breast shall know
Save mine, nor what it is that drives him so,
Backward and forward, in relentless quest.

[The Black Panther]

Andrew Dickson White
(1832-1918)

[p] The cardinal doctrine of a fanatic's creed is that his enemies are the enemies of God.

[The History Of The Warfare Of Science With
Theology In Christendom, 1898]

Walt Whitman
(1819-1892)

[q] There is no god more divine than yourself.

[from Rufus K Noyes, Views of Religion]

[r] I think I could turn and live with animals,
They are so placid and self-contained,
I stand and look at them long and long.
They do not sweat and whine about their condition,
They do not lie awake in the dark and weep for their sins,
They do not make me sick discussing their duty to God.

["Song of Myself"]

Oscar Wilde
(1856-1900)

[s] Medievalism, with its saints and martyrs,
its love of self-torture, its wild passion for
wounding itself, its gashing with knives, and
its whipping with rods -- Medievalism is real

Christianity, and the medieval Christ is the real Christ.

["The Soul of Man Under Socialism"]

[t] I am the only person in the world I should like to know thoroughly.

[Lady Windermere's Fan]

[u] There is no sin except stupidity.

[The Critic as Artist. Part II]

[v] Where there is sorrow there is holy ground.

[De Profundis]

[w] The only way to get rid of a temptation is to yield to it.

[The Picture of Dorian Gray.
Chap. 2]

[x] Truth in matters of religion, is simply opinion that has survived.

[The Critic As Artist, 1891]

[y] To believe is very dull. To doubt is intensely engrossing.

[unsourced]

Robert Anton Wilson
(1932-   )

[z] The Bible tell us to be like God, and then on page after page it describes God as a mass murderer. This may be the single most important key to the political behavior of Western Civilization.

[Right Where You Are Sitting Now]

Thomas Wolfe
(1900-1938)

[a] If a man has a talent and cannot use it, he has failed. If he has a talent and uses only half of it, he has partly failed. If he has a talent and learns somehow to use the whole of it, he has gloriously succeeded, and won a satisfaction and a triumph few men ever know.

[The Web and the Rock. Chap. 30]

Mary Wollstonecraft
(1759-1797)

[b] ...the being cannot be termed rational or virtuous, who obeys any authority, but that of reason.

[A Vindication of the Rights of Woman, 1792]

William E. Woodward
(1874-1950)

[c] Vanity as an impulse has without a doubt been of far more benefit to civilization than modesty has ever been.

[George Washington. Chap. 5, Part 1]

William Wordsworth
(1770-1850)

[d] Because the good old rule
Sufficeth them, the simple plan,
That they should take, who have the power,
And they should keep who can.

[Rob Roy's Grave. Stanza 9]

Sir Henry Wotton
(1568-1639)

[e] Lord of himself, though not of lands;
And having nothing, yet hath all.

[The Character of a Happy Life. Stanza 6]

Elinor Hoyt Wylie
(1887-1928)

[f] In masks outrageous and austere
The years go by in single file;
But none has merited my fear,
And none has quite escaped my smile.

[Let No Charitable Hope. Stanza 2]

Thomas Russell Ybarra
(1880-1971)

[g] A Christian is a man who feels
Repentance on a Sunday
For what he did on Saturday
And is going to do on Monday.

[The Christian]

William Butler Yeats
(1865-1939)

[h] The darkness drops again; but now I know
that twenty centuries of stony sleep
Were vested to nightmare by a rocking cradle,
And what rough beast,
        its hour come round at last,
Slouches toward Bethlehem to be born?

["The Second
Coming"]

Israel Zangwill
(1864-1926)

[i] Let us start a new religion with one com-
mandment, 'Enjoy thyself.'

[unsourced]

[j] In how many lives does Love really play a dominant part? The average taxpayer is no more capable of a "grand passion" than of a grand opera.

[Romeo and Juliet and Other Love Stories]

Frank Zappa
(1940-1993)

[k] The whole foundation of Christianity is based on the idea that intellectualism is the work of the Devil. Remember the apple on the tree? Okay, it was the Tree of Knowledge. "You eat this apple, you're going to be as smart as God. We can't have that."

[unsourced]

[l] ...They tried to make me go to Catholic school, too. I lasted a very short time. When the penguin came after me with a ruler, I was out of there.

[unsourced]

[m] My best advice to anyone who wants to raise a happy, mentally healthy child is: KEEP HIM OR HER AS FAR AWAY FROM A CHURCH AS YOU CAN.

[unsourced]

Credits

I would like to thank Robert A. Lang for opening up his personal library to me for additional quotes and for taking the time to find many more quotes himself. He is a true man among men and not only deserves credit but also a place in the body of this work.

Credit also goes to the shadowy figure who goes by the name of "Bill M." Whether it was checking Carlin sources, providing a handful of quotations for this book, or being supportive of TBoSQ since its first edition, he certainly earns mention on this page.

And last, but certainly not least, I would also like to recognize both Blanche Barton and Peter H. Gilmore for inspiring me to create so much of the media I've released under the banner of Purging Talon all of these years. I am so fortunate to have them as friends and they more than merit their own sections in TBoSQ.

Index

(Purely out of convenience, many words and names have been grouped under their respective general categories. If a specific word is not found, try looking under an assumed general category. Letters following page numbers are in reference to page position. Letters run from a to z throughout this book, not a to z on each page.)

Architecture: 3l, 121e, 208q
Aristocracy: 82h
Aristotle: 114h
Arms / Armed: 19l, 137k
    [see also: Gun, Pistol, Rifle]
Arrogance: 125b, 138p
Art(s): 3l, 61g, 76g, 103k, 168f, 169l,
    187o, 208q
Ascension: 110o
Assertiveness: 118u
Association: 38z
Astrology: 52s, 138p
Astronomy: 74t, 141e, 208q
Atheism: 7l, 11t, 13e, 14j, 16v, 24p, 42d,
    46r, 68o, 68q, 87a, 90t, 91y,
    96b, 114g, 150y, 185h
Atonement: 132p, 180i
Attack(ed): 94p, 141c
Attention: 84p
Attis: 20n
Attraction: 166v
Attribute: 129b
Audience: 84p, 124w
Augury: 138p
Author(s): 24m, 76e
Authority: 11s, 12w, 44j, 71i, 138n,
    216d, 220b
Autocrat: 111y
Autonomy: 75d, 90s, 91w, 98l, 160q,
    170v, 183x
Average: 69t, 82h
Aversion(s): 94t
Bad: 31s, 106x, 133x, 217m
    [see also: Evil]
Balaam: 105r
Balance: 177v, 188v
Banner(s): 201p
Baptism: 144v
Battle(s): 138o
Bear-baiting: 137h
Beast(s): 138m, 167d
Beauty: 100q, 123p, 130j, 178b
Beelzebub: 193b
Beggar(s): 206i
Belief(s): 1b, 1c, 5x, 7k, 14j, 17x, 19i,
    20r, 21u, 22y, 28e, 29h, 30j,

38b, 38c, 40n, 42b, 42c, 43f,
    44n, 46p, 48z, 49c, 49d, 50j,
    52p, 52r, 55g, 59a, 68o, 68q,
    70c, 71j, 73r, 80a, 83j, 87z,
    87d, 88e, 88f, 93k, 95v, 98o,
    100r, 100u, 101z, 102a, 102d,
    106x, 108h, 111w, 111x, 111z,
    114g, 118u, 118v, 119y, 120b,
    129w, 131n, 143r, 144w, 145z,
    146e, 146h, 147l, 147m, 152r,
    158e, 158g, 163k, 172w, 173c,
    176m, 179d, 179h, 183v, 183w,
    183z, 184c, 184e, 185j, 186m,
    186n, 187s, 190y, 192p, 193w,
    195m, 197r, 197s, 197t, 198x,
    201o, 203z, 209y, 212j, 215x,
    216b, 216c, 219y
    [see also: Disbelief, Faith]
Bell(s): 173b
Belly: 65b
Bequeath(ing): 199e
Berlin: 176n
Best: 21w, 25r, 82h, 98k
    [see also: Better]
Bestiality: 195k
Bethlehem: 221h
Better: 148q [see also: Best]
Bible, The: 7k, 12x, 13g, 14i, 19k, 43e,
    44j, 44k, 46o, 47u, 59y, 73q,
    74w, 74x, 80d, 83k, 86v, 86w,
    89j, 90p, 97i, 100s, 105r, 106y,
    107b, 108f, 132r, 133v, 141a,
    144s, 150y, 161v, 165p, 180i,
    180j, 182r, 186n, 195l, 197s,
    200m, 208r, 209v, 214q, 216b,
    219z [see also: New Testament,
    Old Testament]
Bigfoot: 3m
Bigotry: 48b, 107y, 139r
Biology / Biological: 98j, 102b
Bird(s): 95w
Birth / Born: 28c, 180i, 204d
Black: 34i, 150c, 169k
Black Friday: 20n
Blame: 96z, 178x
Bland: 126f

Church(es): 1b, 37v, 51o, 67l, 69w, 77k,
    83i, 87a, 105r, 106w, 106x,
    111w, 118t, 118u, 132p, 137i,
    142k, 149x, 150y, 161x, 165r,
    176p, 180j, 183y, 202u, 208q,
    212h, 215v, 222m
    [see also: Sunday School]
Church of Satan: 14m, 77n, 121d, 124z,
    157b, 166w
    [see also: Satanism]
Churchyard(s): 191m
Circumstance(s): 192r
Civilization / Civilized: 17a, 19j, 40p,
    43i, 57s, 70e, 73p, 106s, 107c,
    130k, 146f, 147l, 204c, 220c
Clergy: 57s, 75b, 107y, 111w, 120a,
    139r, 190y, 198w
    [see also: Priest]
Clothes: 193b
Cockroach(es): 145b
Code: 29g
Coercion: 109n
Coin: 39k, 196n
Collective: 179e
College: 64t, 107y
Colonize: 97f
Comfort: 15q, 127m, 142k
Commandment(s): 198b
Common(ality): 122m, 170v, 208n
Common Man/People: 144w, 190c
Common Sense: 143n, 144w, 175i
Communication: 121f
Communion: 149x
Community: 56n
Companion(s): 3k
Compassion: 133z, 202w
Competition: 197r
Complacency: 125b
Complex(ity): 15q, 51l, 51o
Comrade(ship): 90o
Concentration: 17c
Concern: 166w [see also: Care]
Conditioning: 194f
Confidence: 126g, 133u, 162c
Conformity: 127l
Congregation: 212j

Conjecture(s): 111z
Conquer(or): 79t, 79u, 133u, 167d, 170s,
    170t, 183x
Conscience: 96z, 131o, 151f, 151l
Consequence(s): 107d
Conservative: 182t
Consistency: 55i
Consolation: 76f
Conspiracy: 123o
Constitution: 139s
Consumer(ism): 168f
Contagion: 191m
Contempt(ible): 137j
Contradiction(s): 64v, 86v, 89k, 165p,
    208r
Control: 124x, 125d, 143q, 154u, 167d,
    181n, 203x
Convention: 17y, 29g
Conversation: 3k
Conversion: 114g, 123t, 152p
Conviction(s): 143r
Cooperation: 190a
Corporate: 124v
Corpse: 46t
Corrupt(ion): 75c, 92e, 107y, 160o,
    161x
Cosmetics: 126f
Country: 185f
Courage: 17c, 94m, 133y, 147o, 162e,
    186k
Court(s): 187o
Cow: 147n
Coward(ice): 94o, 154u
Cradle: 221h
Cream: 72m
Create / Creation(s): 22b, 129w, 177v
Creationism: 8n, 51n, 80d, 149v
Creation Science: 88h
Creator: 1b, 93k, 198x, 209t
    [see also: God]
Credulity: 96e, 118t
Creed(s): 4u, 28c, 41u, 62p, 96a, 105q,
    110s, 212j, 218p
Crime(s): 69z, 107b, 120z, 177r, 194h
Critic(s) / Criticism: 37x, 77j, 97i, 109k,
    143l, 148u

Glove(s): 161v
Gluttony: [see: Eat]
Goal(s): 15o
Goat of Mendes: 121f
God(s): 1a, 1b, 1c, 6a, 6b, 6f, 6g, 12x,
 12y, 13b, 13c, 13d, 13g, 14j,
 18e, 19i, 20o, 20q, 20r, 22y,
 24l, 24p, 25u, 28e, 30i, 32x,
 34d, 35m, 36u, 38f, 40n, 42z,
 42d, 43g, 46p, 46q, 46s, 47v,
 48z, 49c, 49d, 50h, 50k, 51l,
 51n, 51o, 52q, 52r, 53y, 54a,
 54c, 56n, 57q, 59a, 60b, 60d,
 60e, 61j, 64y, 64z, 65a, 65b,
 67i, 68o, 68p, 68q, 70e, 71f,
 77j, 80b, 83j, 83k, 84m, 86w,
 86y, 87z, 88e, 89k, 90o, 91u,
 92a, 96b, 96c, 96e, 97f, 98l,
 100s, 100u, 102g, 105q, 106t,
 108h, 109k, 109m, 110r, 110u,
 111x, 111y, 112e, 114g, 115j,
 116q, 118v, 118w, 120z, 120b,
 121c, 126f, 130j, 132p, 132q,
 132s, 133u, 140z, 141b, 141d,
 143m, 143n, 143r, 145c, 146f,
 149x, 151l, 154s, 155y, 157a,
 161a, 164l, 172w, 172z, 174e,
 174f, 175g, 177u, 180k, 180l,
 184b, 185g, 185i, 185j, 186l,
 186n, 188u, 188x, 192p, 193z,
 193a, 193d, 194f, 195k, 196p,
 198y, 199d, 201n, 201p, 203z,
 205f, 205g, 205h, 208r, 209s,
 209t, 209x, 211d, 212g, 214m,
 214p, 215r, 218p, 218q, 218r,
 219z, 222k [see also: Christ,
 Creator, Deity, Jesus]
Gold: 2h, 178b
Golden Rule: 192v
Good: 21w, 22a, 31s, 51m, 69u, 94t,
 106x, 131o, 133x, 134b, 138n,
 154u, 168h
Good-For-Nothing: 199f
Goodguy Badge: 182r
Goshen: 61i
Gospel(s): 29f, 54b, 72o, 183a, 187r,

212i
Gossip(s): 124v
Govern(ment): 33a, 36t, 100t, 111w,
 185f, 206i
Grave: 112e, 119x
Great(ness): 89l
Greece: 103k
Greed: 124v
Greek(s): 110s, 158h, 199d, 208q, 216c
Group(s): 173c
Guess(work): 215u
Guidance: 216d
Guilt: 96a, 186n
Gullible: 77k
Gun(s): 132t, 178x
 [see also: Arms, Pistol, Rifle]
Habit(s): 134e
Hallelujah: 106x
Halo: 216e
Happiness: 3k, 40s, 88e, 100q, 104l,
 123t, 127m, 140z, 148q, 169o,
 194i, 196p, 215y
Harlot: 192p
Harm(ing): 17a
Harmony: 92c
Hatred: 18f, 106x, 116o, 124v
Havoc: 191k
Headache: 148p
Hear(ing): 91z
Hearsay: 166x
Heart(less): 112d, 142g
Heat: 152q
Heaven(s): 7l, 13c, 22c, 28d, 31q, 49g,
 59x, 75c, 79z, 83j, 87d, 108h,
 115i, 150b, 159m, 174f, 188x,
 190z, 200m, 204e, 209w, 212g
Hebrew: 132r
Hell: 7l, 18d, 30i, 31q, 49g, 59x, 108h,
 115i, 132p, 148h, 150b, 150c,
 150d, 174f, 176o, 191m, 194e,
 196p
Help(ing): 84r, 116o
Herd, The: 17y, 68n, 125d, 133z, 139q,
 142h, 158d
 [see also: Crowd, Masses]
Hereafter: 79z, 115i [see also: Afterlife]

Here and Now: 194g [see also: Present]
Heresy: 14m, 24o, 42d, 73r, 74u, 103i
Heretic: 37w, 106w
Hero(es): 77j, 94o, 208n
Hierarchy: 47w, 162f
Higher: 103h
Higher Man: 39j, 129w
    [see also: Over-Man]
Himself / Herself: 220e [see also: Self]
History: 5y, 16u, 73p, 75c, 80d, 85s,
    154t, 157b, 170p
Holocaust: 174f
Holy: 22a, 87z, 95x, 219v
Holy Spirit/Ghost: 174f, 177s, 212g
    [see also: God, Christ, Jesus]
Home / House: 56m
Homer: 170s
Homogenization: 15p
Honor: 143n, 147o
Hoodwink: 176m
Hooey: 148p
Horse-hair: 145x
Horus: 29f
House: 43h, 142j
Howth: 112e
Human(ity): 33z, 133x [see also: Man]
Humanism: 16v, 86y, 157c
Humanitarian(ism): 161x
Humankind: [see: Man]
Humble: 31u
Humor(ous): 123r, 124u
    [see also: Laughter]
Hunt(er/ed): 3j, 128q
Hurt: 122i
Hype: 166x
Hypocrisy: 100t, 106u, 107y, 109n, 165s
Hysteria: 125d, 132p, 177s
I: 174e [see also: Self]
Ice Capades: 35m
Iceland: 22y
Icon(s): 14l, 38z
Iconoclasm: 97g
Idea(s): 68q, 85s, 112a, 179d, 179h,
    182t
Ideal(s): 126g
Identity: 84p, 118u, 124z

Idiocy / Idiot: 178b, 193y, 216c
Idol(atry): 18h, 71i, 97h, 100u, 176o
Ignorance: 4u, 8m, 12z, 35l, 48b, 49e,
    51n, 79w, 96c, 96d, 96e, 106s,
    108f, 111v, 128r, 134c, 145x,
    166t, 177s, 206l, 214o, 216d,
    217g
Ill(ness): 146e
Ill-constituted: 160u
Illiterate: 38f, 39g
Illogic(al): 17x, 146e
Illusion(s): 29g, 66g, 104l, 130i, 185j
Image(ry): 84o, 84p
Imaginary: 50h
Imagination: 34d, 56o, 87z, 132p
Immaculate Conception: 110o
Immoral(ity): 147k
Immortal(ity): 30j, 32y, 95v, 119y, 209y
Impression: 26x
Imprison(ed): 109n
Improbable: 146e
Improvement: 128s
Inadequacies: 50h
Incapable: 21w
Incompetence: 186n
Inconsistency: 115m
Ind: 150z
Independence: 36u, 71i, 142h, 205g
Indies: 112b
Indifference: 51m
Indignation: 71l, 216e
Indispensible: 75d
Individual(ist): 62r, 78p, 145b, 190z
Indivisible: 167y
Indulgence: 17z, 191i
Ineptitude: 123n
Inequality: 98j, 130g, 162f
    [see also: Equality]
Inertia: 79x
Infant(s): 88e
Infection: 212f
Inferior(ity): 126i, 127o, 128r
Infidel: 106w
Infinite: 61h
Influence: 73q, 178w
Information: 26x, 200m

Ingersoll, Robert: 87z
Inhumanity: 92f
Iniquity: 116s, 177r
Initiative: 133y
Injustice: 14n, 50h, 74w
    [see also: Justice]
Innocence: 140y
Innovation: 37x
Inquiry: 50i, 80c, 105q, 106s, 163i
    [see also: Question]
Inquisitor: 85s
Insanity: 107b
Insecurity: 116o, 124v
Inspiration: 107c, 108f
Instinct(s): 53u, 62n, 129y, 168e, 178w
Instruction: 129c
Integration: 118u
Integrity: 20o
Intellect(ualism): 22a, 62p, 70d, 86v,
    108j, 115k, 131n, 176q, 222k
Intelligence: 4u, 33a, 48b, 83k, 91z, 94q,
    104o, 118t, 167z, 178b, 183x,
    183a, 186k
Intelligent Design: 51o
Intelligentsia: 145a
Interest(s): 123q, 125a
Internal: 130f
Intervention: 8p, 186n
Intolerance: 92f, 112a
Invention: 107c, 206m
Investigation: 97i, 105q, 106s, 106u,
    197r
Invisible Man: 35n
Invisible War: 124x
Iron: 92g
Isaac: 43g
Isis: 29f
Islam: 3m, 88f, 211d
Jail: 56m
James, William: 183v
Jealous(y): 43g, 209s, 211d, 216e
Jericho: 105r
Jerusalem: 92f
Jester: 125e
Jesus: 3m, 24l, 36r, 38e, 87d, 106x,
    110o, 110q, 118t, 120z, 154s,

163h, 180i, 188x, 194h, 195m,
    211b [see also: Christ, God]
Jew(ish): [see: Judaism, Semite]
Jihad: 88f
John Doe: 147m
Jonah, Captain: 105r
Joseph: 177s
Jostle: 36o
Joy(s): 20p, 22z, 58w, 162e, 174e
Judaism: 19k, 23j, 39h, 54a, 110s, 136f,
    165r, 211d [see also: Semite]
Judge(s): 6d
Judgment: 82f, 95u, 106x, 111z, 115m,
    154s, 206l
Jungle: 116r, 175l
Jupiter: 20r, 110q
Jurisprudence: 103k
Justice: 13d, 37y, 92b, 141d, 147o, 157c,
    202w [see also: Injustice]
Justification: 84m, 154u
Keep(er): 128r, 192p, 220d
Kid(s): [see: Child]
Kill(ing): 30o, 70e, 185f, 211b, 212i
    [see also: Murder, Slaughter]
King(s): 22d, 30k, 39i, 53t, 72n, 92a,
    105q, 191n
Kitten: 181o [see also: Cat]
Knave(ry): 170r
Kneel(ing): 25q, 155y, 215t
Knot: 104n
Knowledge: 2d, 7i, 11r, 12z, 13h, 16u,
    21u, 32x, 34h, 35j, 36q, 37v,
    37x, 49e, 76h, 78o, 93l, 95v,
    96c, 106t, 107c, 111z, 112b,
    118t, 131n, 138n, 147o, 158e,
    159k, 161z, 172z, 174d, 180j,
    185f, 188v, 214o, 214q, 215s,
    219t, 222k
Koran, The: 176q, 216b
Labor: [see: Work]
Laboratory: 146d
Lackey: 47w [see also: Enslavement,
    Servitude, Slave]
Ladder: 103h
Laity: 139r
Latin: 87d

Passion(s): 5w, 54z, 89l, 170v, 192t, 222j
Past: 16u, 112a, 187p
Patience: 58u, 202w
Path: 154u
Patriotism: 193y
Pattern(s): 52s
Payment: 133y
Peace: 136f, 157c, 174e, 199h, 215y
Pendulum: 14n
Penguin(s): 89i, 222l
People: 7k, 14n, 17y, 24m, 28b, 44j,
    60c, 68r, 79y, 84n, 84q, 94r,
    95w, 107y, 111w, 123n, 124v,
    132s, 142g, 168e, 169l, 172w,
    179e, 179h, 204c [see also:
    Human, Man, Society, Woman]
Perception: 179f
Perdition: 141d
Performer(s): 123o, 124w
Perish: 41x, 190d, 202s [see also: Death]
Persecution: 64v, 139r
Perseverance: 91u, 91v, 91w
Perspective(s): 92d, 94t, 176n
Pertinence: 125a
Perversion: 110p
Pet(s): 209t
Pew(s): 105r
Pharnaces Ponticus: 170t
Phenomenon: 146d
Philistine: 180i
Philosophy: 11t, 37y, 54e, 114h, 126j,
    140z, 144w, 157b, 197t
Pious: 127k
Pistol: 215y [see also: Arms, Gun, Rifle]
Pit: 91u
Plane: 88g
Platitude(s): 61i
Plato: 114h
Play(ing): 101y
Pleasure(s): 77j, 134b, 206j
Plumage: 104m
Pocket(s): 109m
Pod People: 168e
Poet(ry): 203x, 209u
Point of View: [see: Perspective]
Poison: 18g

Polar Bear(s): 89i
Police: 100t
Politics / Political: 2d, 47w, 67l, 77n,
    82f, 92e, 103k, 124v, 143p,
    148p, 149v, 183w, 219z
Polyglot: 155x
Poor: 133y
Pope: 174f, 201r [see also:
    Roman Catholic Church]
Popular(ity): 94q, 101w, 122i, 125c,
    125d
Population: 60c, 139t
    [see also: Overpopulation]
Position: 94m
Posterity: 2i, 199f
Potential: 121f
Power: 11r, 15r, 18h, 37x, 47w, 76f,
    84n, 84o, 90s, 95u, 123p, 159l,
    220d
Practical: [see: Pragmatism]
Pragmatism: 17z, 17c, 194g
Praise: 76e, 126h, 143l
Prank(s): 21t, 38a, 168i, 169j, 203y
    [see also: Trick]
Prattle: 100r
Pray(er): 1b, 6e, 18f, 21v, 31t, 36t, 52q,
    60b, 62p, 64z, 67k, 100u, 105r,
    115j, 120b, 131l, 132p, 186l,
    191f, 192p, 193a, 199d, 205h,
    209t, 214m
Preach(ing/er): 59z, 61i, 74u, 86w, 197v
Prejudice: 174f, 217g
Preparation: 181p
Present: 66g, 200l
    [see also: Here And Now]
Preservation: 95u, 175l
President: 89j
Press: 100t
Pretense(s): 145x
Prey: 3j
Price: 162c
Pride: 162e, 174e, 188t [see also: Vanity]
Priest(s): 4r, 22z, 90q, 106v, 109l, 111v,
    118t, 148t, 177s, 193a, 193d,
    199d, 200k
Prince: 138n, 188u

Resolve: 133u
Resourceful(ness): 152m, 192r
Respect: 93l, 96e
Responsibility: 60b, 71g, 77n, 96z, 122j,
    195j, 200l
Resurrection: 20n, 30j, 38e, 110o, 112d,
    154s
Revelation: 17z, 57q, 165q
Revenge: 84q
Reverie: 125b
Revolution(s): 15o, 35j, 138p
Reward(s): 47w, 107d, 198x, 204b, 213l
Rich: 133y [see also: Wealth]
Rifle: 181p, 215y
    [see also: Arms, Gun, Pistol]
Right(s): 111w, 127k, 128u, 154u, 176n,
    178a, 204d
Rivalry: 149x
Riverbed(s): 113f
Robbery: 206i
Rocking Chair: 131l
Rogue(ry): 93i, 109n
Role(s): 84p
Roman Catholic Church: 202u, 217g,
    222l [see also: Pope]
Romantic (period): 206m
Rome: 20n, 103k, 110s, 137k, 212h
Ross, Betsy: 217l
Rule(s) / Ruler: 6b, 142k, 155w, 190c,
    192v
Ruthless(ness): 181o
Sacred: 4t, 182t
Sacrifice(s): 6e, 54c, 77j, 95y, 149x,
    162c
Sadism: 132p
Safe(ty): 13h, 17y, 62l, 69v, 137k, 142k
Saint(s): 13b, 101v, 111v, 164m, 174f,
    218s
Saïs: 29f
Salvation: 28c, 106x, 133w, 159l, 196p,
    215x
Samson: 105r
Sanity: 178x
Santa Claus: 1b, 52r, 67k, 198z
Satan: 12x, 12z, 14m, 14n, 16v, 16w,
    18d, 37v, 37w, 120z, 121d,

121f, 146g, 150z, 150c, 166w,
    190z, 205g, 206m, 208p
    [see also: Devil, Lucifer,
    Prince of Darkness]
Satanic: 15r, 77j, 128u, 157b
Satanism: 14m, 14n, 16t, 16v, 17z, 17b,
    17c, 77m, 77n, 122h, 124z,
    125c, 126j, 128v, 129x, 157b,
    158e, 167c
    [see also: Church of Satan]
Satanist(s): 14l, 15o, 15q, 15s, 17x, 41u,
    69z, 77m, 77n, 121d, 124z,
    125c, 127p, 157b, 157c, 158d,
    158e, 166w, 167b, 167c
Satirist: 35j
Satisfaction(s): 146f
Savage: 199d
Savior(s): 77m, 111m, 121g
Sceptic: 195l [see also: Skepticism]
School(s): 15p, 44j, 55h, 57s, 62r, 83i,
    100t, 107y, 142k, 187o, 222l
Schoolmaster: 101x, 106s
Science: 4s, 8m, 8q, 17z, 18d, 24l, 37y,
    49e, 51l, 51o, 59x, 60d, 61g,
    61i, 71k, 80c, 82e, 83k, 103k,
    106t, 107y, 107c, 120b, 131n,
    145x, 147i, 149v, 149w, 158h,
    163i, 177t, 184d, 187q
Scripture(s): 73s, 133w
Scrutiny: 148u
Sect: 67l, 110t
Secular: 120b
Security: 215y
Seed(s): 202w
Seek(ing): 127p, 141b
Self(-): 3k, 16t, 31r, 77j, 95y, 101v,
    118u, 125b, 126g, 128s, 129x,
    160q, 162c, 175l, 179c, 191l,
    202t, 206m, 218s, 219t
    [see also: I]
Selfishness: 118u, 125e, 194i
Sell(ing): 126f
Sense(s): 11t, 147o, 148p, 172x
Sentence: 64u
Sentiment(ality): 8q, 29g, 178z
Semite: 175i [see also: Judaism]

About The Editor

Matt G. Paradise is Executive Director of Purging Talon, a Satanic media company responsible for releasing groundbreaking and often imitated audio, video, print, and Web work since 1993, including the internationally respected Satanic magazine, *Not Like Most*. Paradise is also a Magister in the Church of Satan and, since the early-1990s, has also done media representative work for the CoS through all major media forms -- network television, radio, print publications, and the Internet. He is the author of *Bearing The Devil's Mark*, a collection of writings on Satanism.

Also From Purging Talon

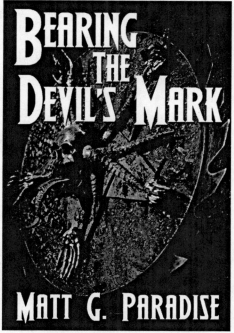

ISBN: 978-0-6151-7668-0

"[Bearing The Devil's Mark] is a well-wrought and welcome volume!
[The author] emerges from these gathered musings as a starkly misanthropic
curmudgeon, and [his] tart observations are just the proper lashes deserved by
the objects of [his] attention. Bravo!"
- Peter H. Gilmore, High Priest of the Church of Satan
and author of The Satanic Scriptures

"...in this entire book there is not a single moment when [the author's] perception
was off in the slightest way... [he has the] ability to explore the Satanic
philosophy and convey nuances of it with the utmost clarity and precision. It's all
absolutely spot-on, like a pure high note held by a world famous opera star."
- Peggy Nadramia, High Priestess of the Church of Satan

www.purgingtalon.com

LaVergne, TN USA
31 March 2011

222350LV00002B/71/P